STUDY GUIDE

Christianity in America

Stephen J. Nichols

LIGONIER MINISTRIES
Renew your Mind.
LIGONIER.ORG | 800-435-4343

421 Ligonier Court, Sanford, FL 32771
E-mail: info@ligonier.org

Printed in China.

Contents

Introduction

Is it necessary to understand the history of Christianity in America to live faithfully today? In this teaching series, Dr. Stephen J. Nichols surveys the history of Christianity in America so that American Christians might know their past and steer a course for the future. The past can help us face the challenges of the present, reminding us about the costs of cultural accommodation but also helping us look back to the cross of Jesus Christ, that we might faithfully proclaim the gospel in the future.

This study guide is a companion to the video teaching series. Whether you are using the DVDs, streaming the videos on Ligonier.org, or going through the course in Ligonier Connect, this resource is designed to help you make the most of the learning experience. For each message in the series, there is a corresponding lesson in this guide. Here is what you will find in each lesson:

INTRODUCTION	The introduction is a brief paragraph that summarizes the content covered in the lecture and considered in the study guide lesson. **How to use:** Use the introduction to each lesson to get a sense of the big picture before watching the video. Refer to these statements as you work through the study guide to remind yourself of what you have already covered and where you are headed.
LEARNING GOALS	The learning goals are the knowledge and skills that the study guide lesson will endeavor to equip you with as you work through the lecture content. **How to use:** Familiarize yourself with the goals of each lesson before engaging its contents. Keeping the overall purpose in mind as you watch each video and reflect on or discuss the questions will help you get the most out of each lesson.
KEY IDEAS	The key ideas are the major points or takeaways from the lecture. **How to use:** Use these ideas to prepare yourself for each lesson and to review previous lessons. They describe specifically the knowledge that each lecture is communicating.

REFLECTION & DISCUSSION QUESTIONS	The questions are the guided reflection and/or discussion component of the lesson that is intended to help you prepare for, process, and organize what you are learning. **How to use:** Reflect on individually or discuss in a group the questions in the order in which they appear in the lesson. The time stamps in the right margin indicate where the answers to questions during the video can be found.
PRAYER	The prayer section offers suggestions for how to close the lesson in prayer with respect to what was taught in the lecture. **How to use:** Consider using each lesson's prayer section as a guide to personal or group prayer. These sections follow the ACTS prayer model, which you can learn more about in R.C. Sproul's Crucial Questions booklet *Does Prayer Change Things?* This helpful guide is available as a free e-book at Ligonier.org.
REVIEW QUIZ	The review quiz is a set of six multiple-choice questions that appears at the end of each lesson. **How to use:** Use each quiz to check your comprehension and memory of the major points covered in each lecture. It will be most beneficial to your learning if you take a lesson's quiz either sometime between lessons or just before you begin the next lesson in the study guide.
ANSWER KEY	The answer key provides explanations for the reflection and discussion questions and answers to the multiple-choice questions in the review quiz. **How to use:** Use the answer key to check your own answers or when you do not know the answer. Note: Do not give in too quickly; struggling for a few moments to recall an answer reinforces it in your mind.

Study Schedules

The following table suggests four plans for working through the *Christianity in America* video teaching series and this companion study guide. Whether you are going through this series on your own or with a group, these schedules should help you plan your study path.

	Extended 14-Week Plan	Standard 12-Week Plan	Abbreviated 6-Week Plan	Intensive 4-Week Plan
Week	**Lesson**			
1	*	1	1 & 2	1–3
2	1	2	3 & 4	4–6
3	2	3	5 & 6	7–9
4	3	4	7 & 8	10–12
5	4	5	9 & 10	
6	5	6	11 & 12	
7	6	7		
8	7	8		
9	8	9		
10	9	10		
11	10	11		
12	11	12		
13	12			
14	*			

* For these weeks, rather than completing lessons, spend your time discussing and praying about your learning goals for the study (the first week) and the most valuable takeaways from the study (the last week).

1

A Tale of Two Paths

INTRODUCTION

How does understanding church history contribute to a Christian's understanding of the present? Is it necessary to understand the roots of Christianity in America in order for Christians to live faithfully in their present age? In this lesson, Dr. Nichols tells the fascinating story of Christianity in America, complete with many interesting characters. However, to understand this story, it is necessary to go back much further than the founding of America.

LEARNING GOALS

When you have finished this lesson, you should be able to:

- Identify the two paths the church tends to take
- Describe the roots of Christianity in America

KEY IDEAS

- American Christianity is a tale of two paths; understanding these two paths ought to produce greater faithfulness to God and His Word.
- The constant interplay between the church and culture in America helps explain Christianity in the context of the United States.
- Christians ought to be countercultural because they are called by God to be "a peculiar people."
- American Christianity finds its roots in the Reformation.

REFLECTION & DISCUSSION QUESTIONS

Before the Video

What Do You Think?

Take a moment to answer the following questions. They will prepare you for the lecture.

- What is your general understanding of Christianity in America, both past and present?
- Why do you think it is important to study the history of Christianity in America? What do you hope to gain from this study?

Scripture Reading

The nations rage, the kingdoms totter; he utters his voice, the earth melts . . . "Be still, and know that I am God. I will be exalted among the nations, I will be exalted in the earth!"

—Psalm 46:6, 10

- Although nations "rage" and "totter," what hope does the Christian have?

During the Video

Answer the following questions while you watch the video. They will guide you through the lecture.

A Tale of Two Paths Explained *0:00–12:21*

- Where does the idea of "a tale of two paths" come from?
- What is "cultural accommodation"?
- What is "confessional affirmation"?

The Roots and History of American Christianity *12:21–24:38*

- What group held sway over Christian identity in early Colonial America?

- Name three key characters from America's church history.

- What are the roots of American Christianity?

After the Video

Answer the following questions after you have finished the lecture to help you identify and summarize the major points.

- Consider Philip Schaff's words from 1844: "Every theological vagabond, every peddler comes here to drive his trade without passport or license and sell his false ware at pleasure. What is to come of such confusion is not now to be seen." How have you experienced the confusion Schaff predicted?

  If you are in a group, share what came to mind about the current state of the American church upon hearing Schaff's words. Discuss any confusion you've seen or felt.

- Augustine wrote *City of God* in the 400s amid the fall of Rome to remind Christians of their need to stay focused on God rather than their culture. How applicable is this idea today compared to the time in which Augustine addressed the matter?

  If you are in a group, discuss the two paths of "cultural accommodation" and "confessional affirmation." How have you seen "cultural accommodation" in the American church? Have members share the allure of this path and how Christians can stand firm as "a peculiar people."

- Dr. Nichols gave an overview of the shifts throughout America's church history. Summarize the various periods from Puritanism to the present.

  If you are in a group, discuss what period or cultural impact was most surprising to you. Share with the group what most impacted you as you listened to Dr. Nichols' overview.

PRAYER

Commit what you have learned from God's Word in this lesson to prayer.

- Praise God for His sovereignty over "tottering" nations and the furtherance of the gospel.
- Confess where you have given in to "cultural accommodation."

- Thank God for His faithfulness to His church and your opportunity to know Him.
- Ask God to equip and empower you to stand firm as "a peculiar people" for His glory.

REVIEW QUIZ

Use these multiple-choice questions to measure what you learned from this lesson.

1. Who was the father of American church historians?
   a. Philip Schaff
   b. John Winthrop
   c. John Owen
   d. George Whitefield
2. What is another name for nominal Christianity?
   a. Confessional affirmation
   b. Countercultural Christianity
   c. Cultural Christianity
   d. American Christianity
3. What New Testament phrase refers to Christians and carries the idea of Christians being countercultural?
   a. Fidelity to Scripture
   b. Faithful disciples
   c. A peculiar people
   d. People of conviction
4. According to Dr. Nichols, what is the importance of studying church history?
   a. It is of little value because Christians should only study the Bible.
   b. It allows Christians to maintain some kind of influence over culture.
   c. It enables Christians to debate with historians about the historicity of Christianity.
   d. It creates more faithful disciples and a more faithful church.
5. Where does the story of American Christianity begin?
   a. In the Reformation
   b. In America
   c. With the Great Awakening
   d. With evangelicalism
6. All of the colonies were settled by branches of the Reformation except one. What was the only colony established as a haven for Roman Catholics?
   a. New York
   b. Maryland
   c. Pennsylvania
   d. New Jersey

Answer Key—A Tale of Two Paths

REFLECTION & DISCUSSION QUESTIONS

Before the Video

What Do You Think?

These are personal questions. The answers should be based on your own knowledge and experience.

Scripture Reading

- Although nations "rage" and "totter," what hope does the Christian have?

  This passage of Scripture reminds the Christian that even though disasters strike in the form of warring and falling nations, God is greater and more powerful. He speaks and the earth "melts" at the sound of His voice. It is not the absence of difficult events in the world that enables the Christian to be still and rest; rather, it is the presence of God and resting in His power over such events. Nothing happens outside of His control, and this gives the Christian great hope.

During the Video

A Tale of Two Paths Explained

- Where does the idea of "a tale of two paths" come from?

  The idea of "a tale of two paths" comes from Augustine's City of God, *in which he contrasts the city of man with the city of God. Augustine encourages believers to maintain a role in their earthly city while not losing sight of their true heavenly home, fixing their focus on God and trusting His rule over the nations.*

- What is "cultural accommodation"?

  Cultural accommodation is what happens when Christians attempt to adapt Christianity to the cultural traditions of the day. It is sometimes motivated by a desire to influence the culture, but Christians often end up being guided and governed by culture rather than the Word of God. The result is a loss of biblical conviction.

- What is "confessional affirmation"?

  Confessional affirmation is submission to God's Word as the governing authority in the Christian's life. This brings about deep convictions, which result in countercultural Christianity as Christians live out their identity as "a peculiar people" who believe and live entirely different than the surrounding culture.

The Roots and History of American Christianity

- What group held sway over Christian identity in early Colonial America?

  The New England Puritans held sway over Christian identity in early Colonial America. They came out of Puritanism in England and dominated the scene in the colonies as they began settling in America in 1620. Puritanism *is an umbrella term that covers several prominent groups.*

- Name three key characters from America's church history.

  Dr. Nichols described Christianity in America as a fascinating story with fascinating characters. Some of the key characters introduced here include Jonathan Edwards, George Whitefield, Timothy Dwight, Charles Grandison Finney, and Billy Graham.

- What are the roots of American Christianity?

  American Christianity is rooted in the Protestant Reformation. All the branches of the Reformation came to America. These branches were represented by the Europeans who came to America from various countries, bringing with them their spiritual beliefs.

After the Video

- Consider Philip Schaff's words from 1844: "Every theological vagabond, every peddler comes here to drive his trade without passport or license and sell his false ware at pleasure. What is to come of such confusion is not now to be seen." How have you experienced the confusion Schaff predicted?

  This is a personal question; the answer should be based on your own knowledge and experience. One potential answer may include the charismatic movement and current trends from Bethel Church.

- Augustine wrote *City of God* in the 400s amid the fall of Rome to remind Christians of their need to stay focused on God rather than their culture. How applicable is this idea today compared to the time in which Augustine addressed the matter?

  Augustine's ideas are equally as applicable today as they were in the 400s. Just as believers during Augustine's day needed to be reminded of the need to hold fast to the Word of God and to keep an eternal perspective, Christians in America need the same reminder today. Believers need to rest in the belief that God is ruling over America with all her divisions and instabilities. The same God who was in control of "tottering" nations in the 400s is in control of "tottering" nations today.

- Dr. Nichols gave an overview of the shifts throughout America's church history. Summarize the various periods from Puritanism to the current state of society.

  Puritanism dominated throughout the early formation of the Colonies but gave way to decline and "half-way" Christianity. This resulted in the Great Awakening.

Then, the early republic was born out of the Revolutionary War, which greatly affected the church. The Second Great Awakening then came about. It was followed by a rise in modernism, which led to liberalism. The church then responded with fundamentalism and evangelicalism. Since about 2000, American Christianity can be described as post-evangelical.

REVIEW QUIZ

1. **A.**
   Philip Schaff was in the German Reformed Church but was an American church historian and an American scholar.

2. **C.**
   Nominalism is the idea of being something in name only. When someone is a nominal Christian, they have pronounced themselves a Christian by default. They have moved from convictions to cultural accommodation, turning to "cultural Christianity."

3. **C.**
   Christians are not Christian by default but by conviction of beliefs. The result of such convictions is countercultural Christianity. God's Word calls Christians to believe differently than the culture on all matters (e.g., marriage, work, humanity, etc.). This produces what the New Testament calls "a peculiar people" because they are different from the surrounding culture.

4. **D.**
   Studying church history enables the Christian to learn from the past in order to better understand the present. This produces Christians who are able to be faithful disciples in their current day. If individual disciples are faithful, it will produce a faithful church that is able to put God's Word and glory on display.

5. **A.**
   The roots of American Christianity are found in the Reformation. It's important to recognize that the American church is a result of God's graciousness and His faithfulness to build His church through the continued proclamation of the gospel "to the end of the earth" (Acts 1:8).

6. **B.**
   The original thirteen Colonies were settled by groups who came out of the Reformation; the Roman Catholic Church had very little presence in the Colonies and was largely confined to Maryland. Due to settlement by the Spanish, Roman Catholicism was dominant in other regions of America and played a greater role later.

2

Puritanism

INTRODUCTION

Many Christians today are familiar with the Puritans and their writings. Among the general population, the Puritans are well known thanks to history and various works of literature, but are they understood in the proper light? In this lesson, Dr. Nichols explores Puritanism, shedding light on its true system of beliefs in order that Christians might understand this foundational movement of American Christianity.

LEARNING GOALS

When you have finished this lesson, you should be able to:

- Explain the core convictions held by the Puritans
- Name several key individuals and their contributions to both Puritanism and society

KEY IDEAS

- There are many stereotypes of Puritans that need to be examined against the truth of who the Puritans were, what they believed, and how they lived their lives.
- Puritanism was marked by a high view of God that led to worship of God in all aspects of life.
- The Puritans were rich in their theology and study of God's Word.
- The Puritans had a lasting impact on society through their love and promotion of learning.

REFLECTION & DISCUSSION QUESTIONS

Before the Video

What Do You Think?

Take a moment to answer the following questions. They will prepare you for the lecture.

- What are your perceptions of the Puritans, and what are those perceptions based on?
- Are you able to articulate the specific beliefs of Puritanism? If so, what are they?

Scripture Reading

Blessed be the God and Father of our Lord Jesus Christ, who has blessed us in Christ with every spiritual blessing in the heavenly places, even as he chose us in him before the foundation of the world, that we should be holy and blameless before him. In love he predestined us for adoption as sons through Jesus Christ, according to the purpose of his will, to the praise of his glorious grace, with which he has blessed us in the Beloved.

—Ephesians 1:3–6

- How does this passage describe the work of salvation in a person's life, and what response should this produce?

During the Video

Answer the following questions while you watch the video. They will guide you through the lecture.

Key Beliefs *0:00–19:42*

- What are the common stereotypes of Puritans, and where do these stereotypes come from?
- In Puritan churches, the pulpits were prominent and elevated. What was the twofold purpose of this?
- What did the notion of covenant govern in the lives of the Puritans?
- In addition to God's Word, what else did the Puritans love to explore?

Key Individuals *19:42–24:24*

- What was Isaac Newton's goal in studying science?

- For what purpose did John Eliot believe God brought the Puritans across the Atlantic?

After the Video

Answer the following questions after you have finished the lecture. They will help you identify and summarize the major points.

- What were the key elements of Calvinism to which the Puritans held fast?

  If you're in a group, discuss how these doctrines can influence your worship of God.

- What were some of the key beliefs held by the Puritans? Can these beliefs be separated from one another?

  Consider these weighty theological beliefs. If you are in a group, discuss where you might struggle in your understanding or practice of these beliefs.

- Dr. Nichols discussed several key Puritans, including John Winthrop, Cotton Mather, Anne Bradstreet, and John Eliot. Name some of the things they were known for and the legacies they left. Were you surprised by any of the legacies left by these Puritans?

  If you are in a group, discuss what surprised you and why. How would you like to be remembered?

PRAYER

Commit what you have learned from God's Word in this lesson to prayer.

- Praise God for His sovereignty, holiness, and transcendence.
- Confess the areas in your life where you have not lived in worship of God.
- Thank God for teaching you deep theological truths that shape your daily living.
- Ask God to grow your understanding of His nature and character that you might better worship Him.

REVIEW QUIZ

Use these multiple-choice questions to measure what you learned from this lesson.

1. According to Dr. Nichols, what is the meaning of the expression *puritanical*?
   a. "Someone who loves God devoutly"
   b. "Someone who is stuffy, rigid, and strict"
   c. "Having to do with Puritanism"
   d. "Having to do with Puritan writings"
2. What distinction does Dr. Nichols make regarding the Puritans' beliefs?
   a. Their beliefs were convictions that got played out in daily living.
   b. Their beliefs did not align with Reformed theology.
   c. They had a very low view of God and a high view of man.
   d. They confessed their beliefs but did not practice them.
3. According to Dr. Nichols, the Puritans were God-centered due to a high view of three attributes of God. Which of the following was *not* included?
   a. Sovereignty
   b. Holiness
   c. Transcendence
   d. Faithfulness
4. What belief dominated the First Great Awakening but was rejected in the Second Great Awakening?
   a. Calvinism
   b. Sufficiency of Scripture
   c. Governance by covenant
   d. Synergism
5. Who wrote the first American church history book?
   a. Increase Mather
   b. Cotton Mather
   c. John Cotton
   d. John Winthrop
6. John Eliot translated several works into Algonquin. Which of the following was *not* one of his works of translation?
   a. The Westminster Shorter and Larger Catechism
   b. The New Testament
   c. The Old Testament
   d. Anne Bradstreet's poetry, *The Tenth Muse*

Answer Key—Puritanism

REFLECTION & DISCUSSION QUESTIONS

Before the Video

What Do You Think?

These are personal questions. The answers should be based on your own knowledge and experience.

Scripture Reading

- How does this passage describe the work of salvation in a person's life, and what response should this produce?

  This passage describes God's beautiful, sovereign work in salvation, as He is the One who has chosen and predestined His sons and daughters. Salvation is a work of God; not of man. The response of the Christian should be one of awe and worship. This passage contains statements about the believer's identity—blessed, chosen, holy, blameless, loved, predestined, and adopted. The believer can rest in this identity secured by Christ and strive to live in light of it.

During the Video

Key Beliefs

- What are the common stereotypes of Puritans, and where do these stereotypes come from?

  Puritans are often considered to be self-righteous hypocrites who are stuffy, rigid, and strict. They are thought of as people who had no fun and didn't approve of others having fun. Some of the contributors to these stereotypes mentioned by Dr. Nichols include Nathaniel Hawthorne's The Scarlet Letter, *Arthur Miller's play that analyzed the Salem Witch Trials, and H.L. Mencken's words regarding the Puritan view of fun.*

- In Puritan churches, the pulpits were prominent and elevated. What was the twofold purpose of this?

  One purpose was for the acoustics. Raising the pulpit allowed people of all ages anywhere in the building to hear the sermon in a time when microphones were not yet invented. More importantly, it was symbolic of coming to church to sit under the authority of the preached Word of God.

- What did the notion of covenant govern in the lives of the Puritans?

  Covenants were very important to the Puritans. Covenants governed every aspect of life, including one's relationship with God, family, church, and society. There was no relationship untouched by covenant.

- In addition to God's Word, what else did the Puritans love to explore?

  The Puritans loved exploring God's world because they loved learning. Education was extremely important to them, and many had studied at Oxford or Cambridge before arriving in America. They quickly founded Harvard University, where students were required to write original poetry. They also loved nature and science. They took seriously the call to live all of life in worship to God, which motivated them to learn about God's world.

Key Individuals

- What was Isaac Newton's goal in studying science?

  Newton studied science and how the world works to gain an even grander vision of the greatness of God and the creation that He gave us. To Newton, studying science was an act of worship; and, as a result, it increased knowledge of God and love for Him, which produced even greater worship.

- For what purpose did John Eliot believe God brought the Puritans across the Atlantic?

  Eliot believed God brought the Puritans across the Atlantic to bring the gospel to the Algonquins. Eliot had a passion for sharing the gospel with this people group and devoted himself to translating works into their language. He was known as the "apostle to the Indians."

After the Video

- What were the key elements of Calvinism to which the Puritans held fast?

  The Puritans were Calvinists. They believed in the total depravity of man—that every person is dead in their transgressions and sins. Because of total depravity, the Puritans believed that salvation is through faith in Christ and is solely the work of God. Salvation as a work of God alone is known as "monergism."

- What were some of the key beliefs held by the Puritans? Can these beliefs be separated from one another?

  The Puritans believed in the importance of worship, God's Word, Calvinism, covenant, and learning. These beliefs are quite difficult to separate from one another since they are intertwined. Every aspect of life was seen as an act of worship to God. A love for and submission to God's Word led to a deep understanding of God and a high view of Him; this produced greater worship of God in addition to firm convictions regarding Calvinism and covenants. Because the Puritans knew God to be the Creator, they loved learning about His world and prized education. As Dr. Nichols described, Puritanism is best understood as a whole system because God was central in everything.

- Dr. Nichols discussed several key Puritans, including John Winthrop, Cotton

Mather, Anne Bradstreet, and John Eliot. Name some of the things they were known for and the legacies they left. Were you surprised by any of the legacies left by these Puritans?

John Winthrop shaped the Pilgrims before they even landed on New England soil when he preached about the perspective of creating a Bible commonwealth in a way that would uphold authority and the respect of people in society. He was a politician and became a governor. Cotton Mather was a prolific thinker and writer, producing books on numerous topics ranging from hermeneutics to astronomy to theology. Out of his quest to worship God, he explored God's world. Anne Bradstreet wrote poetry and applied her Puritan theology to that poetry as she wrote on vulnerable topics such as loss. John Eliot had a heart to share the gospel with the Algonquins and translated the Bible into their language, along with other theological resources. The answer to the second part of the question should be based on your own knowledge and experience. Perhaps you were surprised to discover such a wide variety of contributions.

REVIEW QUIZ

1. **B.**
   Puritanical *is an expression in popular American culture that demonstrates disdain for the Puritans, as it refers to someone who is stuffy, rigid, and strict.*

2. **A.**
   Dr. Nichols referred to confessional affirmation, which he explained in the previous lesson. He describes how Puritanism was not simply a set of beliefs; rather, it was a set of convictions. These convictions worked themselves out in the Puritans' daily living in every aspect of life.

3. **D.**
   The Puritans were God-centered people who had a very high view of God, including His sovereignty, holiness, and transcendence. It is clear from their beliefs and how they lived that this understanding of God's character truly affected every part of them.

4. **A.**
   Calvinism was strong during the First Great Awakening due to the influence of Puritanism. But by the Second Great Awakening, there was a shift away from Calvinism and a complete rejection of it by some of the major figures of that time. Calvinism was replaced by synergism, the idea that salvation is a cooperative effort between God and man; some even went so far as to say the ultimate decision is in the hands of the individual.

5. **B.**
   Dr. Nichols described Cotton Mather as a "stalwart Puritan." Mather wrote Magnalia Americana Christi, *the first American church history book. It details various*

events to convey what God was doing through the Puritans.

6. **D.**
   John Eliot translated the Westminster Shorter and Larger Catechism, the Old Testament, and the New Testament into the Algonquin language. The Algonquin Bible was the first Bible to be published in America.

3

Half-Way Christianity

INTRODUCTION

It may be surprising to note the timeline of the First Great Awakening. After all, why would the First Great Awakening be necessary on the heels of the rich theology and robust Christian living we saw from the Puritans? In this lesson, Dr. Nichols examines the primary contributing factors that led to the decline of early American Christianity and the need for revival.

LEARNING GOALS

When you have finished this lesson, you should be able to:

- Articulate the primary contributing factors that led to the decline of American Christianity after Puritanism
- Understand how easy the drift into nominalism can be
- Identify the faithful individuals God used to prepare the way for the First Great Awakening

KEY IDEAS

- Small compromises in doctrine and practice lead to cataclysmic shifts away from the truth.
- There is no place for "half-way" Christianity in the church.
- Faithful individuals can be used mightily by God if they are willing to stand firmly on His truth.

REFLECTION & DISCUSSION QUESTIONS

Before the Video

What Do You Think?

Take a moment to answer the following questions. They will prepare you for the lecture.

- What do you think contributed to the decline of the church after it had been strongly established in Puritanism?
- Why do you think it's important to learn about this decline?

Scripture Reading

Therefore let anyone who thinks that he stands take heed lest he fall.

—1 Corinthians 10:12

- In the midst of Paul's warning against idolatry and the example of the Israelites, he pens these words. How does this verse apply to Christians and to churches today?

During the Video

Answer the following questions while you watch the video. They will guide you through the lecture.

The Decline *0:00–15:22*

- What did Dr. Nichols say is the pattern of American Christianity, institutions, denominations, and churches?
- What three things contributed to the decline of American Christianity at this time according to Dr. Nichols?
- Describe the move to nominalism that occurred through the Half-Way Covenant.

Precursors to the First Great Awakening *15:22–24:29*

- Why was the Log College established by William Tennent?

- What was the main issue that Theodore Frelinghuysen, William Tennent, and Gilbert Tennent were addressing in the 1720s and early 1730s?

- What did Jonathan Edwards do once he became the minister of the second largest church in America, and what did it produce?

After the Video

Answer the following questions after you have finished the lecture. They will help you identify and summarize the major points.

- When Dr. Nichols described the typical pattern of decline, drift, and eventually apostasy in American Christianity, what came to mind? Have you experienced this with individuals, churches, or institutions? What's necessary to prevent it?

  If you are in a group, discuss how we can guard against this pattern in our own lives.
- Why was Solomon Stoddard open to non-church members' partaking of the Lord's Supper? Are there any areas where you might personally be willing to compromise for similar motives?

  If you are in a group, discuss how something like this might take place in churches today.
- Jonathan Edwards chastised his church for their materialism but not for their prosperity. What is the difference between prosperity and materialism?

  If you are in a group, discuss the problem with materialism that Dr. Nichols described Edwards speaking against. Share with the group any areas where you may be tempted to fall into materialism.

PRAYER

Commit what you have learned from God's Word in this lesson to prayer.

- Praise God for how He raises up faithful men and women who stand on the Word of God.
- Confess any areas of compromise in your own heart and life.
- Thank God for the people in your life who have helped you continue in sound doctrine and practice.

- Ask God to preserve His church from decline, drift, and apostasy.

REVIEW QUIZ

Use these multiple-choice questions to measure what you learned from this lesson.

1. What was the timeline of events in the early years of the American church?
   a. Puritanism, decline, the First Great Awakening
   b. Decline, Puritanism, the First Great Awakening
   c. The First Great Awakening, decline, Puritanism
   d. Puritanism, the First Great Awakening, decline
2. What event damaged New English Puritanism in the early 1690s?
   a. The Inquisition
   b. Witch trials in Europe
   c. Samuel Sewall's apology
   d. The Salem Witch Trials
3. What was the compromise that occurred as a result of the Half-Way Covenant?
   a. Unconverted adults were being baptized
   b. Infants of unconverted parents were being baptized
   c. Unconverted individuals were participating in communion
   d. Infants of converted parents were being baptized
4. The Puritans were known for a lack of desire for awakening.
   a. True
   b. False
5. What did the Log College later became known as?
   a. Yale
   b. Harvard
   c. Princeton
   d. Philadelphia College
6. In England during this time, which two men were preaching against "half-way" Christianity and were kicked out of Anglican pulpits as a result?
   a. John Wesley and George Whitefield
   b. Jonathan Edwards and George Whitefield
   c. Jonathan Edwards and John Wesley
   d. George Whitefield and Gilbert Tennent

Answer Key—Half-Way Christianity

REFLECTION & DISCUSSION QUESTIONS

Before the Video

What Do You Think?

These are personal questions. The answers should be based on your own knowledge and experience.

Scripture Reading

- In the midst of Paul's warning against idolatry and the example of the Israelites, he pens these words. How does this verse apply to Christians and to churches today?

  These words ought to be a sobering reminder to Christians of their daily need for humility and utter dependence on the Lord and His grace. It is easy as believers with strong doctrine to look back at examples from history—be it the Israelites several thousand years ago or the Puritans a few hundred years ago—and to think we would never follow the same path of decline and movement away from God and His truth. Paul's words remind us that we need Christ. We need the ordinary means of grace to saturate our souls and keep us humble and tender toward Him.

During the Video

The Decline

- What did Dr. Nichols say is the pattern of American Christianity, institutions, denominations, and churches?

  Dr. Nichols described the pattern as one of decline, drift, and apostasy. This resulted in the need for the First Great Awakening not long after the high views of God held to and lived by the Puritans.

- What three things contributed to the decline of American Christianity at this time according to Dr. Nichols?

  The Salem Witch Trials, "half-way" Christianity (including the Half-Way Covenant and Stoddardianism), and materialism contributed to the decline of American Christianity at this time.

- Describe the move to nominalism that occurred through the Half-Way Covenant.

  The Half-Way Covenant was a progression away from doctrine and confessional affirmation. Due to a growing number of unregenerate adult children of the Puritans, the church gave way to cultural accommodation, or cultural Christianity. Rather than conforming culture to doctrine, they began conforming doctrine to fit the culture, capitulating to the desire for infants to be baptized regardless of the regenerate state of the parents. This launched them on a dangerous trajectory of decline.

Precursors to the First Great Awakening

- Why was the Log College established by William Tennent?

  Tennent, a former Church of England minister who converted to Presbyterianism, founded the Log College to train ministers because he was suspicious of Harvard and Yale's lack of religious fervor and zeal.

- What was the main issue that Theodore Frelinghuysen, William Tennent, and Gilbert Tennent were addressing in the 1720s and early 1730s?

  Frelinghuysen, a Dutch minister, believed the Dutch churches were full of unconverted ministers, while the Tennents believed the Congregational and Presbyterian churches were full of unconverted ministers. Gilbert Tennent published a sermon titled "The Dangers of an Unconverted Ministry."

- What did Jonathan Edwards do once he became the minister of the second-largest church in America, and what did it produce?

  Edwards started preaching Calvinism. He emphasized man's dependence on God, regeneration as a divine and supernatural work, and God's being glorified in it all. In response to the preaching of this great doctrine, revivals began taking place.

After the Video

- When Dr. Nichols described the typical pattern of decline, drift, and apostasy in American Christianity, what came to mind? Have you experienced this with individuals, churches, or institutions? What's necessary to prevent it?

  These are personal questions; answers should be based on your own knowledge and experience but should connect conceptually to the main ideas of this lesson. While decline, drift, and apostasy may be our trajectory when left to ourselves, the grace of God can keep us from it, which is why we ought to pray toward those ends.

- Why was Solomon Stoddard open to non-church members' partaking of the Lord's Supper? Are there any areas where you might personally be willing to compromise for similar motives?

  Solomon Stoddard believed that the Lord's Supper is a "converting ordinance," so he wanted non-church members to come to the table that they might come to faith, being exposed to the meal as a means of grace. We too can face the temptation to surrender doctrine for pragmatism or cultural deference. Your reflection on the second question is personal, but an example could include an unwillingness to call sin by its true name or call a person to repentance in a misguided attempt to make that person feel more comfortable.

- Jonathan Edwards chastised his church for their materialism but not for their prosperity. What is the difference between prosperity and materialism?

  The difference between prosperity and materialism has to do with an individual's heart and is a matter of worship. According to 1 Timothy 6:10, "The love of money is a root of all kinds of evil. It is through this craving that some have wandered away from the faith and pierced themselves with many pangs." Being successful and prospering financially is not sinful in and of itself. But when love for money and material things replace one's love for God, there is a worship disorder.

REVIEW QUIZ

1. **A.**
   New England had a strong foundation in Puritanism, but various factors led to the decline that created the need for the First Great Awakening. Decline must be away from something, in this case the lofty theology of Puritanism. But by God's grace, it can also be corrected.

2. **D.**
   Witchcraft had been dealt with in Europe through the Inquisition and witch trials. According to Dr. Nichols, it is estimated that approximately 30,000–60,000 suspected witches were killed in Europe during that time. When witchcraft was supposedly discovered in New England and trials took place, the way it was handled created hysteria. Samuel Sewall, one of the trial judges, wrote an apology for the trials, but the damage had already been done.

3. **B.**
   Rather than continuing in the practice of infant baptism of children born to regenerate parents, the church began baptizing infants if a grandparent was regenerate and a parent was baptized. It didn't matter if the baptized parent was a believer or not.

4. **B.**
   The Puritans were marked by gospel warmth, and as a result of such gospel warmth, they had strong desires for gospel awakening. They wanted people to come to know the Lord. Coldness is an inaccurate stereotype of the Puritans.

5. **C.**
   Built as a simple structure made of logs, the Log College moved across the river from Pennsylvania to a carriage stop between New York City and Philadelphia in a place that later became known as Princeton, N.J. The college's name was changed to The College of New Jersey and then to Princeton.

6. **A.**
   John Wesley and George Whitefield both preached a sermon titled "The Almost Christian," in which they called out the Anglicans for their "half-way" Christianity because it wasn't true Christianity.

4

First Great Awakening

INTRODUCTION

The First Great Awakening occurred from 1739 to 1745. This period of revival, repentance, and growth in early American history was marked by the earnest preaching of God's Word and calling the church to return to confessional affirmation. In this lesson, Dr. Nichols explains the pendulum swings toward extreme positions during the First Great Awakening and describes God's work through the champions of the awakening.

LEARNING GOALS

When you have finished this lesson, you should be able to:

- Understand and explain the extreme emphases during the First Great Awakening
- Articulate Jonathan Edwards' involvement in the First Great Awakening
- Summarize the key issues being addressed in this time of revival

KEY IDEAS

- The First Great Awakening, from 1739 to 1745, was a period of great revival in which God's Spirit was at work regenerating souls and reviving His church.
- Extreme emphases and responses have been typical throughout church history, and it was no different throughout the period of the First Great Awakening.

REFLECTION & DISCUSSION QUESTIONS

Before the Video

What Do You Think?

Take a moment to answer the following questions. They will prepare you for the lecture.

- How would you describe this period in church history based on your prior knowledge of the First Great Awakening?
- How do individuals and churches drift so far from strong doctrine as to need revival?

Scripture Reading

[Moses] said to them, "Take to heart all the words by which I am warning you today, that you may command them to your children, that they may be careful to do all the words of this law. For it is no empty word for you, but your very life."

—Deuteronomy 32:46–47

- What should be the Christian's response to the Word of the Lord?

During the Video

Answer the following questions while you watch the video. They will guide you through the lecture.

The Pendulum Swing *0:00–6:19*

- What were the two extremes of the First Great Awakening that Dr. Nichols referred to, and who were the key characters in each?
- What was Charles Chauncy's purpose in writing *Seasonable Thoughts on the State of Religion in New England*?

The Champions of the Awakening *6:19–24:27*

- What was Jonathan Edwards' purpose in preaching his famous sermon "Sinners in the Hands of an Angry God"?
- What was always Edwards' goal in preaching?
- In contrast to Edwards' impassioned intellect, what did the detractors neglect? What did the fanatics neglect?

- What was George Whitefield's emphasis in his preaching?

After the Video

Answer the following questions after you have finished the lecture. They will help you identify and summarize the major points.

- Consider Dr. Nichols' statement that people tend to go to one extreme or another. Why do you think this is true?

  If you're in a group, discuss areas where you have tended toward an extreme side of an issue. Why was this the case?

- Jonathan Edwards' "Sinners in the Hands of an Angry God" is based on Deuteronomy 32. According to Dr. Nichols, what did Moses anticipate Israel doing? Why do we, even as Christians, tend to forget God in good times?

  If you are in a group, take a few moments to read Deuteronomy 8 and 32 together. Spend a few minutes praying for God's grace to remain humble and dependent in both good and difficult times.

- What did Dr. Nichols say was unique about Edwards as a preacher?

  If you are in a group, discuss whether you tend toward head or heart. What are the dangers of neglecting one of these?

PRAYER

Commit what you have learned from God's Word in this lesson to prayer.

- Praise God for the work of the Spirit to revive souls.
- Confess areas of doctrine and practice where you have overemphasized something to the neglect of another.
- Thank God that His words give warning and that His words give life.
- Ask God to help you "relish" His presence and His Word.

REVIEW QUIZ

Use these multiple-choice questions to measure what you learned from this lesson.

1. Who were the champions of the First Great Awakening?
   a. Jonathan Edwards and George Whitefield
   b. James Davenport and Charles Chauncy
   c. James Davenport and Jonathan Edwards
   d. George Whitefield and Charles Chauncy

2. Why did James Davenport begin sponsoring book burning?
   a. Books were expensive to print at the time, and he believed books were a sign of wealth and extravagance.
   b. He believed reading was a waste of time and people should be preaching and sharing the gospel with others.
   c. He believed books were a distraction from the pure Word of God and that there should be more freedom of the Spirit.
   d. He was influenced by a mentor to begin sponsoring book burning.

3. What effect did "Sinners in the Hands of an Angry God" have on the congregation in Enfield, Conn.?
   a. A great negative effect: the people were angered and kicked Edwards out of town.
   b. No effect: the people were unmoved by the message.
   c. Little effect: some people, but not a significant number, were saved.
   d. A great positive effect: the Spirit was at work and people cried out to God for the salvation of their souls.

4. John Calvin said that saving knowledge of God was *sensus suavitatus*. What does this phrase mean?
   a. "Experience with the senses"
   b. "The five senses"
   c. "Taste and see"
   d. "A sense of sweetness"

5. What did the First Great Awakening produce in the American culture?
   a. It produced a sense of unified Colonial identity.
   b. It produced a further fracturing of unity between colonies.
   c. It produced the American Revolution as a direct result.
   d. There was no impact on the culture.

6. How many people came to Christ through the First Great Awakening?
   a. Approximately 7,000 people
   b. Approximately 15,000 people
   c. Approximately 60,000 people
   d. Approximately 100,000 people

Answer Key—First Great Awakening

REFLECTION & DISCUSSION QUESTIONS

Before the Video

What Do You Think?

These are personal questions. The answers should be based on your own knowledge and experience.

Scripture Reading

- What should be the Christian's response to the Word of the Lord?

  We are to take God's Word and His warnings to heart. This includes believing, obeying, and teaching them. As this passage teaches us, the Word of the Lord and His commands are life to the believer and should be taken in and savored.

During the Video

The Pendulum Swing

- What were the two extremes of the First Great Awakening that Dr. Nichols referred to, and who were the key characters in each?

  Dr. Nichols referred to the fanatics as one extreme. James Davenport was a key figure of this movement. The detractors were on the opposite side of the spectrum, and a significant figure of this movement was Charles Chauncy.

- What was Charles Chauncy's purpose in writing *Seasonable Thoughts on the State of Religion in New England*?

  Chauncy wrote down all the expressions of fanaticism he could find in order to create a catalogue of the worst of side of the First Great Awakening. He did so to diminish and detract from the Great Awakening.

The Champions of the Awakening

- What was Jonathan Edwards' purpose in preaching his famous sermon "Sinners in the Hands of an Angry God"?

  Just as Israel had been unfaithful to their covenant with God, Edwards said the Puritans were being unfaithful to their covenant with God. As a result, he called them to return to covenant faithfulness.

- What was always Edwards' goal in preaching?

  He desired to see people's hearts truly penetrated by the Word and work of God. He wanted the gospel to do its work and to carefully stay clear of temporary emotionalism.

- In contrast to Edwards' impassioned intellect, what did the detractors neglect? What did the fanatics neglect?

  Edwards had an "impassioned intellect"—a healthy, invigorated emotional response to the truth of God, which he taught and defended. The detractors neglected the emotion of the soul, while the fanatics gave in to emotionalism and neglected truth.

- What was George Whitefield's emphasis in his preaching?

  Whitefield focused on regeneration in his preaching in the same way Jesus focused on new birth in His approach with Nicodemus. Jesus told Nicodemus, "You must be born again," a powerful statement that would become the title of one of Whitefield's favorite sermons to preach.

After the Video

- Consider Dr. Nichols' statement that people tend to go to one extreme or another. Why do you think this is true?

  There are various reasons people tend toward extremism. One reason might be pride. If a person is knowledgeable in a certain doctrine and becomes fixated on and passionate about it, they may become proud. Paul warned about knowledge that "puffs up" as opposed to the motivation of love that "builds up" (1 Cor. 8:1). Another reason might be a genuine desire to correct a wrong doctrine. Just as a person driving a car might overcorrect in response to danger, the believer might overcorrect in response to dangerous doctrine and practice.

- Jonathan Edwards' "Sinners in the Hands of an Angry God" is based on Deuteronomy 32. According to Dr. Nichols, what did Moses anticipate Israel doing? Why do we, even as Christians, tend to forget God in good times?

  Moses knew that once the Israelites were in the promised land with abundant provisions and safety, they would begin to rely on themselves and forget their dependence on God. We are no different than the Israelites in this way. Our hearts are bent toward pride and self-sufficiency, and we need constant reminders of who our great God is and who we are—desperate people in need of His mercy and grace.

- What did Dr. Nichols say was unique about Edwards as a preacher?

  Edwards was able to combine both head and heart. He saw doctrine as biblical and rational, but he had passion for the truth and maintained true affection. Just as John Calvin cultivated an appreciation for the sweetness of God and His Word, Edwards maintained a heart that relished his God.

REVIEW QUIZ

1. **A.**
In addition to Edwards, who was already in America, Whitefield came over from England in 1739. These men were some of the major figures that God used in the First Great Awakening, while Davenport and Chauncy represent the extremes of the revival movement.

2. **C.**
Davenport was a leader of the fanatics. He was an agitator, known for stirring things up and creating problems. He claimed that books were a distraction from God's Word; he began sponsoring book burning because he thought there was too much book learning occurring and that there should be a greater emphasis on the freedom and zeal of the Spirit.

3. **D.**
Edwards originally preached "Sinners in the Hands of an Angry God" in Northampton, Mass., where there was little response from the congregation. However, when he preached the sermon in Enfield, Conn., the Spirit of God was at work and people were crying out in repentance.

4. **D.**
The phrase literally means "a sense of sweetness." Calvin described a saving knowledge of God in this way, and Edwards picked up on this idea and focused on relishing God and His Word.

5. **A.**
Before the awakening, people identified themselves by the colony they were from. The revivals brought them together and created greater unity between people across the Colonies.

6. **C.**
The First Great Awakening was a period during which the Spirit of God was at work reviving hearts, and approximately 50,000–70,000 people came to Christ through the revivals of this time.

5

Early Republic

INTRODUCTION

What happened to the church in America and to American culture on the heels of the First Great Awakening? We saw tremendous revival occur between 1739 and 1745, but unfortunately, it did not last. What contributed to this decline? In this lesson, Dr. Nichols explains the distractions and beliefs that took root during the 1700s and 1800s that created a mindset that shifted away from God, the Bible, and the church.

LEARNING GOALS

When you have finished this lesson, you should be able to:

- Describe the church and American culture after the First Great Awakening
- Discuss the significance of the beliefs and doctrinal issues that undermined true Christianity during this time period
- Identify and describe the key figures in addition to their beliefs and/or contributions
- Grasp the importance of holding fast to the deity of Christ and a biblical view of God

KEY IDEAS

- Worldly distractions lead to a lack of commitment to God, His church, and His Word.
- When a lesser view of Christ is held, His deity and the truth of the gospel are diminished.
- God uses faithful saints to accomplish His great purposes.

REFLECTION & DISCUSSION QUESTIONS

Before the Video

What Do You Think?

Take a moment to answer the following questions. They will prepare you for the lecture.

- What internal or external factors contribute to the decline of the church?
- What might easily distract Christians from their faith and the truth of God's Word throughout various periods of history?

Scripture Reading

He is the image of the invisible God, the firstborn of all creation. For in him all the fullness of God was pleased to dwell.

—Colossians 1:15, 19

And if Christ has not been raised, then our preaching is in vain and your faith is in vain. We are even found to be misrepresenting God, because we testified about God that he raised Christ. . . . If in Christ we have hope in this life only, we are of all people most to be pitied.

—1 Corinthians 15:14–15a, 19

- How important are the deity of Christ and His resurrection to the Christian faith?

During the Video

Answer the following questions while you watch the video. They will guide you through the lecture.

The Rise of Deism *0:00–13:28*

- What happened to church attendance during the 1790s, and what phenomenon is primarily to blame?
- What are the three tenets of deism?
- What is the deist view of God?

Other Factors Leading to Revival *13:28-24:06*

- According to Jonathan Edwards, there were two enemies of the American church that gave rise to Unitarian universalism. What were they?
- What are the core beliefs of Unitarian universalism?
- What are the three waves of revival that historians put together and consider to be the Second Great Awakening?

After the Video

Answer the following questions after you have finished the lecture. They will help you identify and summarize the major points.

- While Thomas Jefferson's approach to the Bible may sound absurd, think of the ways this principle is enacted in various religions, Christian churches, and culture. What are some examples you've seen of this?

  If you're in a group, discuss the effects you've seen of picking and choosing portions of God's Word. To take this a step further, consider ways you've done this, perhaps unintentionally, in your own life.
- Deism was the church's cultural accommodation to the influences of the Enlightenment. Briefly explain the Enlightenment—who were the primary philosophers, when did it take place, and what were the results?

  If you're in a group, discuss why accommodating these philosophies may have been appealing to the church at that time.
- What do you think are the affairs of the world today that can distract Christians and challenge their faith commitments?

  If you are in a group, consider and confess the areas where you are tempted to fix your gaze more on the things of earth than on Christ. Discuss how you can grow in setting your mind on things above according to Colossians 3:1–4.

PRAYER

Commit what you have learned from God's Word in this lesson to prayer.

- Praise God for the hope we have in Christ and His resurrection.
- Confess any ways you have been distracted from loving God and loving others.
- Thank God for giving you the divine revelation of His Word.
- Ask God to use you as a light in a dark world in need of the gospel.

REVIEW QUIZ

Use these multiple-choice questions to measure what you learned from this lesson.

1. What took place in America on the heels of the First Great Awakening?
   a. The Revolutionary War
   b. The Second Great Awakening
   c. Puritanism
   d. Intellectualism

2. Who was one of the most famous and most widely read authors among the Americans during the early republic?
   a. William Ellery Channing
   b. Charles Chauncy
   c. Thomas Jefferson
   d. Thomas Paine

3. Who created their own version of the Bible titled "The Words and Works of Jesus Christ"?
   a. William Ellery Channing
   b. Charles Chauncy
   c. Thomas Jefferson
   d. Thomas Paine

4. Why do deists believe general revelation is superior to the divine revelation found in the Word of God?
   a. Natural revelation is more concrete and easier to understand.
   b. Natural revelation is universal and can be accessed by anyone, anywhere.
   c. People did not have access to copies of the written Word of God.
   d. People were unable to read and, therefore, the Bible was inaccessible.

5. What did Timothy Dwight start doing at Yale that God greatly used to stir a revival?
   a. Holding meetings to discuss the differences between Christianity and deism
   b. Listening to the faculty at Yale and debating philosophy
   c. Holding prayer meetings and praying for revival
   d. Defending the Bible as the Word of God and preaching the gospel

6. The revival of the Second Great Awakening was a response to all *except* which of the following?
   a. The decline in American culture
   b. The rise and prevalence of deism and Unitarian universalism
   c. The prosperity and busyness that came through building a nation
   d. The persecution of Christians that took place during the Revolutionary War

Answer Key—Early Republic

REFLECTION & DISCUSSION QUESTIONS

Before the Video

What Do You Think?

These are personal questions. The answers should be based on your own knowledge and experience.

Scripture Reading

- How important are the deity of Christ and His resurrection to the Christian faith?

  The deity of Christ is of utmost importance in the Christian faith. Scripture is clear that Jesus is the Son of God, who is the same in substance and glory with the Father. He is the "image of the invisible God." If Christ were not God, He would not have been the perfect, infinite sacrifice that satisfied God's holy wrath against sin. If we remove the resurrection of Christ from the gospel, we no longer have a gospel. As Paul said, we are without hope if Christ was not raised from the dead.

During the Video

The Rise of Deism

- What happened to church attendance during the 1790s, and what phenomenon is primarily to blame?

  Church attendance declined significantly and was almost nonexistent during the 1790s. The main contributing factor to this was the rise of deism. Deism had become popular among England's elite and eventually made its way over to America. The key figures involved with founding American government and influencing American culture were deists.

- What are the three tenets of deism?

  First, general revelation is superior to Scripture. Second, formal religion is good for morality, and morality is good for society. Third, Jesus is history's greatest moral teacher, but He is not God.

- What is the deist view of God?

  According to the deists, and in contrast with the biblical view of God as holy, God is an essentially benevolent, gracious, and understanding God. Deists believe that while God desires morality and goodness from His creatures, His benevolence makes Him see how our goodness outweighs the bad.

Other Factors Leading to Revival

- According to Jonathan Edwards, there were two enemies of the American church that gave rise to Unitarian universalism. What were they?

  Edwards warned against Arminianism and Arianism and the damaging effects these beliefs would have. It is easy to see how Arminianism, a belief that diminishes God's sovereignty in salvation, and Arianism, the belief that Christ was created and therefore not divine, would lead to the beliefs held in Unitarian universalism.

- What are the core beliefs of Unitarian universalism?

  William Ellery Channing preached an important message that set the tone for the movement. He said that the Trinity was irrational and, therefore, rejected the doctrine of the triune God. He argued that God would be robbed of worship if Jesus and the Holy Spirit were also worshiped. In addition to rejecting the Trinity, Channing believed that God's benevolent love, grace, and mercy are freely available to all, teaching that salvation is universal.

- What are the three waves of revival that historians put together and consider to be the Second Great Awakening?

  Campus revivals beginning in 1802 at Yale spread throughout academic institutions. Before that, in 1801, revival broke out in Cane Ridge, Ky., spreading camp meeting revivals throughout Kentucky, Tennessee, and the Carolinas through the 1830s. The revivalist preaching of Charles Grandison Finney in the 1820s and 1830s is also a mark of the Second Great Awakening.

After the Video

- While Thomas Jefferson's approach to the Bible may sound absurd, think of the ways this principle is enacted in various religions, Christian churches, and culture. What are some examples you've seen of this?

  Thomas Jefferson, true to deist beliefs, cut out the supernatural portions of Scripture to create what came to be known as the Jefferson Bible. In many ways, people still pick and choose what they want to believe from the Bible. One example is to do away with any passages of Scripture relating to gender and gender roles. Often, unpopular or controversial passages of Scripture are ignored or explained away.

- Deism was the church's cultural accommodation to the influences of the Enlightenment. Briefly explain the Enlightenment—who were the primary philosophers, when did it take place, and what were the results?

  Some of the primary philosophers of the Enlightenment were John Locke, David Hume, and Immanuel Kant. The Enlightenment came after the Reformation, spanning from the late 1600s to the 1700s. This era sought to do away with the authority of the church, Christendom, and the Bible.

- What do you think are the affairs of the world today that can distract Christians and challenge their faith commitments?

  The answer to this question should be based on your own knowledge and experience. One answer may be related to wealth and comfort in America. Abundance can easily lead to distraction and preoccupation with the things of this world. People might become so fixated on comfort that they do not recognize their deep spiritual needs because their comfort is preventing them from feeling a desperate need for God.

REVIEW QUIZ

1. **A.**
   After the First Great Awakening, America was in the midst of the Revolutionary War and the building of a nation. It is imperative to understand how this set the stage for the necessity of the Second Great Awakening.

2. **D.**
   Thomas Paine was known for his pamphlets written during the war to encourage the war efforts. After the war, he wrote the book The Age of Reason, *which promoted deism.*

3. **C.**
   Thomas Jefferson took the Bible and literally cut and pasted portions of it to create what would come to be known as the Jefferson Bible. He cut out all the miracles of Christ and any claims of deity in order to get to the moral teachings of Jesus.

4. **B.**
   Since general revelation is readily available to everyone, deists promoted it over and above Scripture. As a result, nature was elevated to a higher position because man could know God more universally through nature. Therefore, God's Word was not seen as a necessary means of communion with God.

5. **D.**
   Timothy Dwight became the president of Yale in 1795. Since the faculty was made up of deists who didn't believe the Bible was the Word of God, Dwight began debating with them. In addition, Dwight began preaching the gospel week after week in chapel for seven years straight. He testified to the fact that God was at work stirring revival in the hearts of the people at Yale.

6. **D.**
   While persecution is often a means that God uses to purify His church and cause revival, that was not seen at this period in time. The need for revival boiled down to the rise in false doctrine and distractions in the culture and the new nation.

6

Second Great Awakening

INTRODUCTION

After the Revolutionary War and the beginnings of a new nation, the Second Great Awakening transpired throughout the early 1800s. The Second Great Awakening occurred at a time when the American people and church were distracted by the things of this world and influenced by various philosophies. In this lesson, Dr. Nichols explains the emphases of this awakening in contrast to the First Great Awakening.

LEARNING GOALS

When you have finished this lesson, you should be able to:

- Describe the events, figures, and characteristics of the Second Great Awakening
- Compare and contrast the First Great Awakening and the Second Great Awakening
- Grasp the importance of cultural and doctrinal influences on the church

KEY IDEAS

- The Second Great Awakening was marked by new measures and Biblicism.
- There were different emphases in the First Great Awakening and the Second Great Awakening.
- God remains faithful to His people and His church, even throughout varying winds of doctrine and practice.

REFLECTION & DISCUSSION QUESTIONS

Before the Video

What Do You Think?

Take a moment to answer the following questions. They will prepare you for the lecture.

- What is your current knowledge and understanding of the Second Great Awakening? How would you distinguish it from the First Great Awakening?

- Are you aware of any influences from the period of the Second Great Awakening on the contemporary Christian church? If so, list some of those influences. If not, think of contemporary Christian church culture and write down some key words or phrases to describe it.

Scripture Reading

O Timothy, guard the deposit entrusted to you. Avoid the irreverent babble and contradictions of what is falsely called "knowledge," for by professing it some have swerved from the faith. Grace be with you.

—1 Timothy 6:20–21

- How have you seen the gospel distorted? Why is it of utmost importance that we guard the truth of the gospel?

During the Video

Answer the following questions while you watch the video. They will guide you through the lecture.

New Measures of Awakening *0:00–15:03*

- Who was Peter Cartwright and why is he significant?

- What was foreshadowed at Cane Ridge that was to come later in the Pentecostal movement in the 1900s?

- What did Dr. Nichols refer to as "new measures," and what was Charles Finney's involvement?

Biblicism and the Contrasting Awakenings *15:03–24:37*

- According to Dr. Nichols, what is the purpose of creeds and confessions?

- What is the fundamental problem with Biblicism?
- What was the biggest contrast between the First Great Awakening and the Second Great Awakening?

After the Video

Answer the following questions after you have finished the lecture. They will help you identify and summarize the major points.

- What are awakenings throughout church history the result of? Has there been a time in your life where you've witnessed revival on a small scale, perhaps in your family, church, or community? Describe that season of revival.

  If you are in a group, discuss your answers to the personal question above in light of the centrality of God's Word.

- Martin Luther said, "The love of God does not find that which is lovely but creates it." What did Luther mean by this?

  If you are in a group, discuss the comfort this statement brings.

- What are some of the ways the Second Great Awakening has influenced contemporary American Christianity?

  If you are in a group, discuss the importance of holding fast to right doctrine and how we, as believers and as individual churches, ought to guard the gospel with which we have been entrusted.

PRAYER

Commit what you have learned from God's Word in this lesson to prayer.

- Praise God that salvation is dependent on Him and not on us.
- Confess areas where you've given in to the influence of the culture or extra-biblical ideas.
- Thank God for the faithful men and women who shared the gospel with you.
- Ask God to help you be faithful to the true gospel and that you would not negotiate or weaken it.

REVIEW QUIZ

Use these multiple-choice questions to measure what you learned from this lesson.

1. What word was used to describe what was taking place at Cane Ridge, Ky.?
   a. Excitement
   b. Enthusiasm
   c. Penitence
   d. Sadness
2. What did the term "soul anxious" refer to?
   a. Anxiety
   b. Conviction
   c. Depression
   d. Sinful fear
3. According to Dr. Nichols, what was the fundamental problem with the Second Great Awakening?
   a. Too many preachers from various denominations came together.
   b. It was too localized and didn't spread far enough in its reach.
   c. There was a negotiating and weakening of the gospel.
   d. The Bible was not used.
4. What is Biblicism?
   a. The idea that Christians ought to study the Bible
   b. The belief that the Bible is God's inerrant Word
   c. The belief that the Bible is the sufficient Word of God
   d. The idea that there is no creed but the Bible
5. Which denomination was founded in the early 1800s by Barton Stone and Alexander Campbell?
   a. Church of Christ
   b. Reformed Presbyterian
   c. Methodist
   d. Church of God
6. The First Great Awakening and the Second Great Awakening were similar in terms of the truths proclaimed and the impact and effects they had.
   a. True
   b. False

Answer Key—Second Great Awakening

REFLECTION & DISCUSSION QUESTIONS

Before the Video

What Do You Think?

These are personal questions. The answers should be based on your own knowledge and experience.

Scripture Reading

- How have you seen the gospel distorted? Why is it of utmost importance that we guard the truth of the gospel?

  The first question is personal and will depend on your experiences. The second question focuses on the importance of the truth of the gospel. In this epistle, Paul urges Timothy to confront false teaching in the church. What is evident in Scripture and in the Second Great Awakening is that if a little error in doctrine is allowed, it will eventually lead to massive shifts and distortions to the gospel. As believers, we must remain true to the gospel, proclaiming it in all purity.

During the Video

New Measures of Awakening

- Who was Peter Cartwright and why is he significant?

  Cartwright was one of the most popular Methodist preachers in the early 1800s. He wrote about the Second Great Awakening and the revival that took place at Cane Ridge, Ky. His diary provides a firsthand account, so we have an accurate understanding of what took place.

- What was foreshadowed at Cane Ridge that was to come later in the Pentecostal movement in the 1900s?

  Enthusiasm was emphasized at Cane Ridge, Ky. It was enthusiasm beyond what we tend to think of as excitement or passion for the things of God. Rather, it emphasized dramatic or uncontrollable physical expression as being part of a genuine religious conversion. This was seen later on in the Pentecostal movement.

- What did Dr. Nichols refer to as "new measures," and what was Charles Finney's involvement?

  Charles Finney was not interested in theological systems; instead, he was interested in being innovative and creating the right environment for revival to take place. These were "new measures." Finney created the "anxious bench," where those who were convicted could come forward in an act that symbolized conversion rather than waiting for a time to seek counsel with the pastor. Finney's innovation involved the use of music and setting the right tone or mood.

Biblicism and the Contrasting Awakenings

- According to Dr. Nichols, what is the purpose of creeds and confessions?

  Creeds and confessions synthesize the teaching of the Bible, helping us bring the whole counsel of God into consideration.

- What is the fundamental problem with Biblicism?

  While Biblicism might sound good on the surface, it can result in people not taking the whole counsel of God into consideration. Rather, the tendency is to focus on passages that one naturally gravitates toward, considering those portions of Scripture in isolation and not weighing passages from other parts of God's Word.

- What was the biggest contrast between the First Great Awakening and the Second Great Awakening?

  The First Great Awakening was confessional and Calvinistic. There was a deep understanding of and emphasis on salvation as a work of God. The Second Great Awakening stressed the work of man and placed the emphasis on man's response to God.

After the Video

- What are awakenings throughout church history the result of? Has there been a time in your life where you've witnessed revival on a small scale, perhaps in your family, church, or community? Describe that season of revival.

  True awakenings are the result of the Spirit of God working through the preaching of God's Word. This makes God's Word central for our analysis of awakening, and this should be taken into consideration when answering the second question.

- Martin Luther said, "The love of God does not find that which is lovely but creates it." What did Luther mean by this?

  Luther was pointing out the truth of the human condition: we are all sinners at the root and enemies of God. According to Dr. Sproul, we have all committed "cosmic treason" since we are rebels against the God of the universe. The fact that God creates that which is lovely rather than looks for it is a demonstration of His grace.

- What are some of the ways the Second Great Awakening has influenced contemporary American Christianity?

  Dr. Nichols pointed to several ways the Second Great Awakening has shaped the contemporary American church. We can see the roots of the Pentecostal movement forming through the emphasis on outward physical expressions being part of one's conversion. In its most obvious form, that is seen today in televangelists and faith healers. The effects of the mood and atmosphere of the church, including altar calls, can still be seen today. Finally, Dr. Nichols stressed the shift from trained ministers to those who were simply gifted in the art of persuasion. This is seen today in the modern attraction to influencers and personalities.

REVIEW QUIZ

1. **B.**
   Enthusiasm *was used to describe the Second Great Awakening due to the dramatic outward expressions that were emphasized in it. This was quite different than the definition typically thought of by the use of the word.*

2. **B.**
   The Puritans used the term soul anxious *to speak of a person who was under conviction when hearing the Word of God preached. The day after the sermon, the "soul anxious" person would send a note to the pastor or elder asking for counsel; the pastor or elder would then call on them at their house and counsel them.*

3. **C.**
   During the Second Great Awakening, the emphasis was on man and his response to God rather than on God's sovereign work in salvation. Finney even rejected the doctrine of original sin, believing man has the capability of posturing himself in a state of acceptance to God. This weakened the gospel message and cheapened God's grace.

4. **D.**
   Biblicism did away with the historic, orthodox creeds and confessions of the faith on the basis of a belief that the Bible was the only thing one needed.

5. **A.**
   Stone and Campbell followed the path of Biblicism and started the Church of Christ, also known as the Disciples of Christ, which was committed to reading the Bible only. The denomination spread rapidly throughout the United States.

6. **B.**
   The First Great Awakening and the Second Great Awakening were, as Dr. Nichols said, a tale of two paths or a tale of two awakenings. The First Great Awakening was confessional and Calvinistic while the Second Great Awakening stressed man's response to God and diminished God's grace and the gospel. Some of the negative effects of the Second Great Awakening are still seen today in the American church.

7

Rise of Liberalism

INTRODUCTION

As we move on from the Second Great Awakening, we find America in a unique period of western expansion and populism. The American church is facing modernism and the question whether it will affirm confessionalism or accommodate the culture. In this lesson, Dr. Nichols explains six contributions to the rise of liberalism in American Christianity.

LEARNING GOALS

When you have finished this lesson, you should be able to:

- Describe modernism, liberalism, and the contributions to the rise of liberalism
- Discuss the significance of cultural accommodations made by the church
- Understand the detriment caused by questioning the authority and inerrancy of Scripture and replacing Scripture with new ideas
- Grasp the origins of the social gospel

KEY IDEAS

- The emphasis on "new measures" or innovations during the Second Great Awakening continued to have an effect throughout the 1800s in both American culture and Christianity.
- While many things contributed to the rise of liberalism over several decades, Dr. Nichols identifies six key contributing factors.

REFLECTION & DISCUSSION QUESTIONS

Before the Video

What Do You Think?

Take a moment to answer the following questions. They will prepare you for the lecture.

- Given where American Christianity left off after the Second Great Awakening, what would you guess was the next major challenge for the American church?
- How would you define *liberalism*?

Scripture Reading

And we have the prophetic word more fully confirmed, to which you will do well to pay attention . . . knowing this first of all, that no prophecy of Scripture comes from someone's own interpretation. For no prophecy was ever produced by the will of man, but men spoke from God as they were carried along by the Holy Spirit.

—2 Peter 1:19, 20–21

- According to this passage, how has God's Word been declared? How does this bring confidence in knowing and understanding God's truth?

During the Video

Answer the following questions while you watch the video. They will guide you through the lecture.

The Church and Cultural Climate 0:00–7:33

- What were the driving forces of American culture from the 1800s to the 1840s?
- How did the desire to move away from the traditional to the new measures and the populist impulse affect the church?
- As Christianity progressed out into the frontier, what was common and what was emerging as a new brand of American Christianity?

Contributions to the Rise of Liberalism *7:33–24:47*

- What did German higher criticism threaten, and how did it primarily make its way into America?
- What did Dr. Nichols identify as the six contributions to liberalism?
- How did the inevitability of progress affect American Christianity?

After the Video

Answer the following questions after you have finished the lecture. They will help you identify and summarize the major points.

- What did the social gospel attempt to do, and what was the result?

  If you are in a group, discuss the dangers of the pendulum's swinging too far in either direction on this issue. What happens if the church only preaches the gospel, and what happens if the church only meets physical needs?
- Dr. Nichols referenced Dr. Sproul's idea that often when you put an "-ism" on the end of a word, it's not a good thing, even if the original thing was good (for example, the difference between piety and pietism). Why is this often true?

  If you're in a group, discuss examples where you may have seen this take place.
- Consider the contributions to liberalism discussed by Dr. Nichols as well as liberalism itself. Are there any ways you have perhaps been subtly influenced by any of these? Do you ever think that something new is better? How do you discern when that mentality is true to reality or prejudiced against it?

  If you are in a group, confess these subtle ways of wrong thinking and pray for the Spirit to give you discernment and steadfast commitment to His truth.

PRAYER

Commit what you have learned from God's Word in this lesson to prayer.

- Praise God for churches that have held fast to the Word of God and confessionalism.
- Confess ways you have adopted unbiblical concepts even in small, subtle ways.

- Thank God for trained pastors and elders and for the opportunity to receive training in God's Word.
- Ask God to give you wisdom and discernment as you navigate current cultural trends and ideologies.

REVIEW QUIZ

Use these multiple-choice questions to measure what you learned from this lesson.

1. What was the impact of the frontier and Jacksonian democracy on American Christianity?
   a. Religious pietism
   b. Religious populism
   c. Christian politics
   d. Christian democracy

2. What was Christianity attempting to accommodate with liberalism?
   a. Modernism
   b. The Enlightenment
   c. Darwinism
   d. Deism

3. What was Christianity attempting to accommodate with deism?
   a. The Revolutionary War
   b. The Enlightenment
   c. Modernism
   d. Liberalism

4. What was the embrace of rationalism a response to?
   a. Churches that had embraced Biblicism
   b. The continued effects of the Enlightenment
   c. Seminaries that had become biblically watered down and weak
   d. The enthusiasm that came out of the Second Great Awakening

5. During what period was the social gospel on the rise?
   a. 1820s–1850s
   b. 1850s–1900s
   c. 1900s–1950s
   d. 1900s to present

6. Americans immediately embraced the ideas in *On the Origin of Species*.
   a. True
   b. False

Answer Key—Rise of Liberalism

REFLECTION & DISCUSSION QUESTIONS

Before the Video

What Do You Think?

These are personal questions. The answers should be based on your own knowledge and experience.

Scripture Reading

- According to this passage, how has God's Word been declared? How does this bring confidence in knowing and understanding God's truth?

  This passage teaches us that God's Word has been declared not merely by men, but by the very work of God through the Holy Spirit. There ought to be great confidence and comfort in knowing that "we have the prophetic word fully confirmed" and that prophecy is not left to "someone's own interpretation" or "produced by the will of man." This creates confidence because we know that God is the author of all truth, and He does not change. We can trust His infinite knowledge, infinite wisdom, and infinite power. People are fickle, constantly shifting and changing. We stand firm, anchored in the unshakable truth of God because His Word is direct revelation from Him.

During the Video

The Church and Cultural Climate

- What were the driving forces of American culture from the 1800s to the 1840s?

  The two primary elements were the frontier and Jacksonian democracy. The Eastern Seaboard had been settled, and there was a push to move westward and settle the Western Frontier, beginning with the Midwest and moving out further west. The Jacksonian democracy was the era when Andrew Jackson, a populist, defeated John Quincy Adams—who represented old Colonial New England—in the presidential election.

- How did the desire to move away from the traditional for the new measures and the populist impulse affect the church?

  The Presbyterians, the Congregationalists, and the Anglicans—the old denominations that had been prevalent throughout the Eastern Seaboard—diminished and declined throughout the 1800s. In the 1790s, Methodism came to America and quickly spread. The Baptists also rose and began to spread.

- As Christianity progressed out into the frontier, what was common and what was emerging as a new brand of American Christianity?

The older denominations valued confessionalism. Their pasters were trained clergy who were well versed in the confessions of the faith; they had gone to seminary and had learned the biblical languages. However, the newer denominations were primarily led by untrained clergy. They were out on the frontier forsaking confessionalism for Biblicism.

Contributions to the Rise of Liberalism

- What did German higher criticism threaten, and how did it primarily make its way into America?

  It threatened biblical authority through questioning such things as the authorship and historicity of the Bible. It primarily came to America through American scholars who were reading books by German higher critics, going to Germany for more education, and training under these German higher critics.

- What did Dr. Nichols identify as the six contributions to liberalism?

  Dr. Nichols identified the following as the key contributions to liberalism: enthusiasm, social activism, German higher criticism, pietism, Darwinism, and the inevitability of "progress."

- How did the inevitability of progress affect American Christianity?

  Progress, as a way of interpreting the world, looks ahead and sees what is newer as better. Therefore, the converse is true: older is worse. When this is applied to God's Word, it undermines the authority and inerrancy of the Bible. It opens the door for everything to be questioned and easily cast aside, which is precisely what modernity did.

After the Video

- What did the social gospel attempt to do, and what was the result?

  In response to a rise in various social problems, the social gospel began out of good intentions to address real people in need and real social crises. The social gospel sought to eradicate poverty, famine, and injustice based on the belief that God's salvation was deliverance from such things rather than deliverance from sin. It was a misapplication of the gospel that ended up redefining and distorting the true gospel.

- Dr. Nichols referenced Dr. Sproul's idea that often when you put an "-ism" on the end of a word, it's not a good thing, even if the original thing was good. Take piety and pietism, for example. Why is this often true?

  If we are to be worshipers of Christ, what happens when we elevate an idea through making it an "-ism"? Oftentimes, there is an over-elevation, and whatever the belief or idea is gets elevated above the actual worship of Christ Himself. It's also easy for the concept to get distorted as time goes on, even if the original intent was beneficial. Often, the principle will be taken beyond what God's Word teaches.

- Consider the contributions to liberalism discussed by Dr. Nichols as well as liberalism itself. Are there any ways that you have perhaps been subtly influenced by any of these? Do you ever think that something new is better? How do you discern when that mentality is true to reality or prejudiced against it?

  This is a personal question, and the answer will vary based on your own personal reflection but should take into consideration some or all of the six contributing factors of the rise of liberalism.

REVIEW QUIZ

1. **B.**
   The era of the frontier and Jacksonian democracy was one of leaving old traditions behind in search of new ones. There was a sense of exploration in the nation geographically as well as ideologically. These ways of thinking took root in the church as old denominations were set aside for new ones.

2. **A.**
   The church desired to maintain cultural relevance. Therefore, in the face of modernism, the church compromised on truth, questioning confessions and creeds along with long-held understandings of Scripture and doctrine.

3. **B.**
   Dr. Nichols has focused throughout this series on how the church tends toward cultural accommodation or confessionalism. The Enlightenment was a period of pursuing freedom from the church, the Bible, and religious authority. The church accommodated the infiltration of these philosophies through deism.

4. **D.**
   The church often struggles with finding a balanced response to issues and tends toward swinging the pendulum too far in the opposite direction. When enthusiasm and excessive emotional expressions dominated the scene, the church overreacted to these excesses with rationalism, emphasizing the need to be thoughtful and educated.

5. **B.**
   Though the social gospel came to its full effect in the 1900s, it was during the 1850s–1900s that the social gospel was on the rise. This was due, in large part, to Walter Rauschenbusch, who is often considered the founder of the movement.

6. **B.**
   Charles Darwin wrote On the Origin of Species *in 1859, which cast a competing worldview that the world was developed through natural forces rather than through a divine Creator. While his ideas would be embraced eventually, it was not until the Scopes Trial in 1925 that the theory of evolution began to hold full sway.*

8

Fundamentalism, Part 1

INTRODUCTION

The early American Christian church was marked by complexity. Consider all that has occurred in the nation up to this point in our study along with the various winds of doctrine and philosophies. What was needed in the church at that particular time of history? In this lesson, Dr. Nichols looks at the strong roots of Princeton Theological Seminary and provides an overview of the beliefs and branches of fundamentalism.

LEARNING GOALS

When you have finished this lesson, you should be able to:

- Explain the faithful positions held at Princeton Theological Seminary
- Discuss the beliefs and branches of fundamentalism
- Grasp the importance of maintaining the tradition of sound doctrine

KEY IDEAS

- Princeton Theological Seminary embraced confessional affirmation and remained strong in sound doctrine for many years.
- When the authority of Scripture is questioned, it opens the floodgates for doubt and skepticism.
- Serious errors arise when the supernatural is questioned and Christianity is reduced to naturalism.
- It is important to not only believe right doctrine but to have firm convictions and to stand on them.

REFLECTION & DISCUSSION QUESTIONS

Before the Video

What Do You Think?

Take a moment to answer the following questions. They will prepare you for the lecture.

- What is your understanding of fundamentalism? Do you have positive or negative associations with it?
- What are the fundamental doctrines of the faith on which you would be willing to take a courageous stand, convinced of their weightiness and validity?

Scripture Reading

Follow the pattern of the sound words that you have heard from me, in the faith and love that are in Christ Jesus. By the Holy Spirit who dwells within us, guard the good deposit entrusted to you.

—2 Timothy 1:13–14

- As you prepare for this lesson, consider the people in your life who have taught you the gospel and shared "sound words" with you. What does it mean "to guard the good deposit entrusted to you," and how is that done?

During the Video

Answer the following questions while you watch the video. They will guide you through the lecture.

Princeton Theological Seminary *0:00–10:56*

- Who was Charles Hodge?
- What did the Princetonians assert against German higher critics?
- What were the five convictions that Princeton upheld?

The Beliefs and Branches of Fundamentalism *10:56–24:54*

- What are the six "fundamentals" that the fundamentalists came to agree on?

- There were different coalitions or branches within fundamentalism. What were they unified on and where did they differ in their beliefs?

- What are the five branches of fundamentalism?

After the Video

Answer the following questions after you have finished the lecture. They will help you identify and summarize the major points.

- Consider Charles Hodge's words: "A new idea never originated at Princeton Theological Seminary." What did Hodge mean by this?

  If you are in a group, discuss: Do you think everything new is bad and leads to heresy? Where do we draw the line as believers when it comes to adopting new ideas or ways of doing things?
- Dr. Nichols touched on Princeton's emphasis on both the head and the heart; he mentioned the idea of "a warm Calvinism." Consider this phrase. What would "a warm Calvinism" look like in contrast to "a cold Calvinism"?

  If you are in a group, discuss whether you have known anyone (perhaps even yourself) who has at first been put off by strong Calvinistic churches based on the perception of coldness. How might the church display greater warmth while holding fast to strong doctrine and teaching?
- Both the Princetonians and the fundamentalists emphasized the supernatural. Why did they believe this was important?

  If you are in a group, discuss: Do you tend to think of Christianity as supernatural or do you tend toward naturalism? Why?

PRAYER

Commit what you have learned from God's Word in this lesson to prayer.

- Praise God for His commitment to faithfully build His church.
- Confess ways that you have reduced your faith to rationalism and left out love and worship for God.
- Thank God for indwelling you by the Holy Spirit and thereby enabling you "to guard the good deposit entrusted to you" (2 Tim. 1:14).

- Ask God to remind you of the supernatural elements of your faith and to keep you from naturalism.

REVIEW QUIZ

Use these multiple-choice questions to measure what you learned from this lesson.

1. What does the Latin word *tradidit*—from which we get the English word *tradition*—mean?
   a. "To hold on"
   b. "To hand over"
   c. "To give up"
   d. "To stay the same"
2. How did Princeton counter both pietism and rationalism?
   a. Through maintaining Congregationalist traditions
   b. Through bringing back the enthusiasm of the Second Great Awakening
   c. Through their vision of combining piety of the heart with solid learning
   d. Through emphasizing the need for training and higher education
3. What was a central tenet of Immanuel Kant's influence?
   a. He made a distinction between knowledge and faith.
   b. He made a distinction between the head and the heart.
   c. He believed that theology was a science.
   d. He did not believe in transcendence.
4. "A fundamentalist is anyone who believes in the fundamentals and is willing to . . ." What completes this quote?
   a. ". . . do battle royal for them."
   b. ". . . take on the German higher critics over them."
   c. ". . . stake their very lives on them."
   d. ". . . start a new church that defends them."
5. What branch of fundamentalism became the largest movement to dominate not only the United States but the world?
   a. Dispensationalism
   b. Separatism
   c. Revivalism
   d. Pentecostalism
6. Dispensationalism began in England. Who was the major propagator of this view in the United States?
   a. John Nelson Darby
   b. Cyrus Ingersoll Scofield
   c. J. Gresham Machen
   d. George Marsden

Answer Key—Fundamentalism, Part 1

REFLECTION & DISCUSSION QUESTIONS

Before the Video

What Do You Think?

These are personal questions. The answers should be based on your own knowledge and experience.

Scripture Reading

- As you prepare for this lesson, consider the people in your life who have taught you the gospel and shared "sound words" with you. What does it mean "to guard the good deposit entrusted to you," and how is that done?

  This is a personal question to help prepare you for some of the material covered in this lesson. The answer should be based on your own knowledge and experience.

During the Video

Princeton Theological Seminary

- Who was Charles Hodge?

  Charles Hodge went to Princeton Seminary and was converted there in 1815. He went on to Germany, where he confronted theological liberalism. He came back from his time in Germany unwavering and even stronger in his positions, and he taught theology at Princeton for many years.

- What did the Princetonians assert against German higher critics?

  The Princetonians stood for biblical authority. They believed the doctrine of inspiration, that the Word of God was God-breathed. Because they believed the Bible was the inspired Word of God, they believed in the inerrancy of the Bible; since God cannot lie, His Word must be true. Based on this, the Princetonians believed in biblical authority, which was contrary to what was espoused by the German higher critics.

- What were the five convictions that Princeton upheld?

  Princeton (1) upheld tradition, (2) focused on piety of heart with solid learning, (3) upheld biblical authority, (4) emphasized the supernatural, and (5) believed in theology as science.

The Beliefs and Branches of Fundamentalism

- What are the six "fundamentals" that the fundamentalists came to agree on?

As a whole, the fundamentalists agreed on (1) the inerrancy of Scripture, (2) the virgin birth, (3) the substitutionary atonement, (4) the bodily resurrection of Christ, (5) the validity of miracles, and (6) the literal second coming of Christ.

- There were different coalitions or branches within fundamentalism. What were they unified on and where did they differ in their beliefs?

  The different groups of fundamentalists all agreed on what they were opposed to. Where they did not agree was how to replace what they were opposed to. Therefore, so long as they agreed on the fundamental or foundational issues of doctrine, they could identify themselves as fundamentalists while maintaining differing positions on certain peripheral areas of doctrine and practice.

- What are the five branches of fundamentalism?

  The five branches of fundamentalism discussed by Dr. Nichols are Pentecostalism, dispensationalism, separatism, revivalism, and confessionalism.

After the Video

- Consider Charles Hodge's words: "A new idea never originated at Princeton Theological Seminary." What did Hodge mean by this?

  According to Dr. Nichols, Hodge and the Princetonians drew on the Apostle Paul's model of handing over and entrusting the gospel ministry to faithful men who would then train other faithful men. The understanding was that the truth of God's Word was timeless and should be passed on from generation to generation. Therefore, Hodge and Princeton remained steadfast in the truth of God's Word without sensing the need to alter it to be relevant for new times and new people.

- Dr. Nichols touched on Princeton's emphasis on both the head and the heart; he mentioned the idea of "a warm Calvinism." Consider this phrase. What would "a warm Calvinism" look like in contrast to "a cold Calvinism"?

  As a way to counter rationalism, which reduced Christianity to thinking and right doctrine, Princeton emphasized the need for both head and heart, just as Jonathan Edwards had taught in the First Great Awakening. Because Calvinism is rooted in rich, solid, deep doctrine, people can sometimes tend to focus solely on the academic side of maintaining right theology. "A warm Calvinism," however, considers the depths of God's love and character behind those great doctrines. As a person sets his or her heart on God's love that pursues rebellious, stubborn sinners, humility and gratitude are cultivated in the heart. The heart ought to warm in response to God's mercy, love, and grace. God is a lavish God who desires our love and worship, not simply our right confessed theology.

- Both the Princetonians and the fundamentalists emphasized the supernatural. Why did they believe this was important?

  Both of these groups had a strong emphasis on the supernatural because God, His works, and Christianity itself are all supernatural. As Dr. Nichols pointed out, the virgin birth was a miracle, the resurrection was a miracle, and Jesus performed miracles throughout His ministry. There is nothing natural about our faith, but deism and liberalism had pushed God out of the world and reduced everything to naturalism and humanism.

REVIEW QUIZ

1. **B.**
   Tradition *can conjure up negative connotations for many people. The Latin word* tradidit, *however, means "to hand over," which carries the idea of passing down truth. This is what Paul had in mind when he entrusted the ministry of the gospel to Timothy.*

2. **C.**
   Archibald Alexander's vision for Princeton was along the same lines as Jonathan Edwards' heartbeat for the Christian. Alexander understood that studying God's Word and gaining knowledge of God was complementary to loving and worshiping God. The focus of the Princetonians was piety of heart in combination with rigorous study and learning. There was no dichotomy of the heart and the head.

3. **A.**
   Kant's central tenet was that science, knowledge, and certainty are diametrically opposed to faith, the supernatural, and the transcendent. The Princetonians opposed this idea with the belief that theology is a science and that faith and knowledge do go together.

4. **A.**
   Fundamentalism was not simply focused on beliefs; this willingness "to do battle royal" for the beliefs was central to the fundamentalists. They had the courage to stand on their convictions and fight for them.

5. **D.**
   Pentecostalism began in 1906 on Azusa Street in California as a reaction to modernism and liberalism, especially the rationalism that came out of liberalism. There was a heavy emphasis on morality as the American culture was drifting further away from its Christian roots. This movement took off and continued to expand throughout the twentieth century all around the world.

6. **B.**
   Cyrus Ingersoll Scofield, a dispensationalist, wrote a study Bible in 1909 that was revised and republished in 1917. The sales of this Bible were so great that they actually kept Oxford University Press from going under during the Great Depression. Through Scofield, the ideas of dispensationalism were popularized throughout the United States.

9

Fundamentalism, Part 2

INTRODUCTION

As we saw in the previous lesson, there were several branches of fundamentalism. Each branch had their own emphasis and influence as they stood against liberalism. In this lesson, Dr. Nichols focuses our attention on the revivalist fundamentalists and the confessional fundamentalists as he explains their faithfulness to the true gospel and the fundamental doctrines of the Christian faith. J. Gresham Machen, a primary figure among the confessional fundamentalists, created a lasting legacy of faith.

LEARNING GOALS

When you have finished this lesson, you should be able to:

- Describe the revivalist fundamentalists and the confessional fundamentalists
- Discuss the significance of J. Gresham Machen's contribution to the church and to society
- Grasp the importance of orthodox Christian doctrine

KEY IDEAS

- The revivalist fundamentalists pushed back against modernism through revival gospel preaching, and the confessional fundamentalists fought liberalism through maintaining traditional views of doctrine.
- J. Gresham Machen had a great influence on the Presbyterian denomination and Christian institutions.
- Doctrine is of utmost importance, and right Christian living flows from right doctrine.
- The church ought to be a place that offers something different than what the world offers.

REFLECTION & DISCUSSION QUESTIONS

Before the Video

What Do You Think?

Take a moment to answer the following questions. They will prepare you for the lecture.

- How did theological institutions such as Harvard, Yale, and Princeton drift so far from the truth? How do we guard against this drift in our institutions today?

- What is your current understanding of J. Gresham Machen, his beliefs, and his contribution to the church?

Scripture Reading

But as for you, continue in what you have learned and have firmly believed, knowing from whom you learned it and how from childhood you have been acquainted with the sacred writings, which are able to make you wise for salvation through faith in Christ Jesus.

—2 Timothy 3:14–15

- What charge did Paul give Timothy? How do we guard against drifting from Christian orthodoxy in our own personal lives?

During the Video

Answer the following questions while you watch the video. They will guide you through the lecture.

The Revivalists and Confessionalists *0:00–12:20*

- What was Billy Sunday known for?

- What did Dr. Nichols indicate may have helped J. Gresham Machen find his purpose?

- Who mentored Machen at Princeton, and what did he wisely tell Machen in response to Machen's idea that the denomination was on the verge of a split?

Fosdick and Machen *12:20–25:00*

- What was the purpose of Harry Emerson Fosdick's 1922 sermon "Shall the Fundamentalists Win?"
- How did Machen explain an orthodox view of Christ?
- Why did Machen open Westminster Theological Seminary?

After the Video

Answer the following questions after you have finished the lecture. They will help you identify and summarize the major points.

- Who were the two revivalist preachers that Dr. Nichols described, and what were their methods of evangelism? What are some practical ways people can use their gift of evangelism today?

  If you're in a group, discuss how these men and their faithful proclamation of the simple gospel message inspires you in sharing the gospel with others.
- Machen maintained that America was a free country in which people are free to believe what they want to believe. Where did he draw the line in people's beliefs when it came to claiming Christianity?

  If you are in a group, discuss how you navigate the beliefs of other Christians who might not agree with you about everything. How do you exercise charity when it comes to certain issues?
- What is the answer to humanity's problems?

  If you're in a group, discuss the ways you see culture and the church today offer solutions to humanity's problems. How can the church be countercultural and offer true hope?

PRAYER

Commit what you have learned from God's Word in this lesson to prayer.

- Praise God that He offers a solution to our deepest problem.
- Confess ways that you have striven for peace and harmony at the cost of funda-

mental convictions.

- Thank God for the faithfulness of Machen and the legacy of right doctrine that has been passed on through his labors.
- Ask God to give you boldness and courage to stand immovable on the truth of His Word.

REVIEW QUIZ

Use these multiple-choice questions to measure what you learned from this lesson.

1. Who began Sunday schools in the urban areas of Chicago?
   a. Harry Emerson Fosdick
   b. J. Gresham Machen
   c. Dwight L. Moody
   d. Billy Sunday

2. J. Gresham Machen went to Princeton reluctantly.
   a. True
   b. False

3. Who was the "poster pastor" for liberalism according to Dr. Nichols?
   a. Billy Sunday
   b. Dwight L. Moody
   c. J. Gresham Machen
   d. Harry Emerson Fosdick

4. What was the purpose of Machen's *Christianity and Liberalism* in 1923?
   a. To expand on a work begun by B.B. Warfield
   b. To proclaim his conservative political views
   c. To refute Harry Emerson Fosdick's rejection of the fundamentals
   d. To pay tribute to Woodrow Wilson's influence on his life

5. What did Machen say that the unregenerate find in the liberal church instead of the answers to the chaos and confusion in the world?
   a. The true gospel
   b. Exactly what's out in the world
   c. A message that made them feel better
   d. A new community

6. Who created the main problems on the board at Princeton in the 1920s and 1930s?
   a. The moderates created the problems.
   b. The liberals created the problems.
   c. The conservatives created the problems.
   d. The moderates, liberals, and conservatives shared an equal part in creating the problems.

Answer Key—Fundamentalism, Part 2

REFLECTION & DISCUSSION QUESTIONS

Before the Video

What Do You Think?

These are personal questions. The answers should be based on your own knowledge and experience.

Scripture Reading

- What charge did Paul give Timothy? How do we guard against drifting from Christian orthodoxy in our own personal lives?

  Paul advised Timothy to continue in the truth he'd already received and learned. Timothy had studied the Scriptures, and he had faith in Christ and salvation as a result. One way we can guard against drifting away from orthodoxy is to be people of the Word. We need to know, study, and meditate on God's Word so that His truth reigns in our minds and hearts.

During the Video

The Revivalists and Confessionalists

- What was Billy Sunday known for?

  Billy Sunday was the successor to D.L. Moody as a dynamic revivalist preacher. He was a professional baseball player turned Presbyterian minister, but his real gifting was as an evangelist. He pushed against modernism and naturalism through the preaching of a simple gospel message.

- What did Dr. Nichols indicate may have helped J. Gresham Machen find his purpose?

  Machen volunteered to serve in World War I. He ran a YMCA canteen, where he would make hot chocolate for the soldiers and hold conversations in between bombs going off. Before this time, Machen seemed a bit uncertain as to his life purpose. Once he returned from the war, he seemed committed to Princeton with a greater fervor and dedicated much of his life to studying, teaching, and defending the truth of God's Word and right doctrine.

- Who mentored Machen at Princeton, and what did he wisely tell Machen in response to Machen's idea that the denomination was on the verge of a split?

  B.B. Warfield mentored Machen during Warfield's final years. When Machen offered his idea that the denomination was on the verge of a split, Warfield replied that the denomination was already too far gone and was beyond repair.

Unfortunately, this proved true, and Machen was involved in much controversy within his own denomination and at Princeton.

Fosdick and Machen

- What was the purpose of Harry Emerson Fosdick's 1922 sermon "Shall the Fundamentalists Win?"

  Fosdick was a liberal who was anti-fundamentalism. The goal of his sermon was to refute the necessity of the five fundamentals for Christianity. In fact, he claimed that Christians should entirely reject those fundamentals.

- How did Machen explain an orthodox view of Christ?

  Machen said: "Any view of Jesus that is less than infinite is infinitely less than the real thing." What he meant by this is that in order to have an accurate view of Christ, one must understand Him to be the God-man. Any view that sees Christ as less than God, no matter how high a view of Christ one might maintain, is not the correct view of Christ as He is portrayed in Scripture.

- Why did Machen open Westminster Theological Seminary?

  Machen was at odds with Princeton as well as with his denomination. After twenty years of serving at Princeton, Machen was no longer welcome there, so he began a new seminary where confessional subscription was primary. He sought to establish a seminary that followed the Princeton of the old days, a place that combined piety of heart with solid learning.

After the Video

- Who were the two revivalist preachers that Dr. Nichols described, and what were their methods of evangelism? What are some practical ways people can use their gift of evangelism today?

  Dr. Nichols described the ministries of D.L. Moody and Billy Sunday. Moody used his service at the YMCA during the Civil War to share the gospel with the troops. Sunday was truly an evangelist and would travel by train from city to city and set up tent revival meetings. Both of these men were revivalists, but they shared something in common that ought to encourage us today: they were faithful to steward and share the gospel. Today, that could look like being intentional in choosing the same cashier at the grocery store in order to build a relationship and create opportunities for the gospel. For another person, it might look like engaging in street preaching or setting up a table at the mall to talk with people about Christ. Maybe for you, it's praying for that wayward family member who's been weighing on your heart and pursuing bold, prayerful intentionality the next time you're together.

- Machen maintained that America was a free country in which people are free to believe what they want to believe. Where did he draw the line in people's beliefs when it came to claiming Christianity?

Machen was quite vocal in his view of freedom in the United States and even people's freedom to believe what they wanted to. However, he was not supportive of people denying the fundamentals of Christian orthodoxy while still calling it "Christianity." Machen wrote Christianity and Liberalism, *in which he explained that Christianity is both a doctrine and a lifestyle, but that it is first a doctrine. In this book, he expounded on who God is, biblical authority, who Christ is, the doctrine of man, the doctrine of salvation, and the church.*

- What is the answer to humanity's problems?

  The answer to humanity's problems is a right understanding of who God is and who we are as humans. When we understand our sinfulness, our separation from the Holy Creator God, and that Christ died, was buried, and rose again in order to reconcile us to God, the root of our problems is resolved. Rather than our problem being social, intellectual, technological, etc., our fundamental problem is theological, so a theological solution is necessary. Humanity's deepest problem can only be answered when we look to God.

REVIEW QUIZ

1. **C.**
   D.L. Moody saw children in the urban areas of Chicago who were directionless. He decided to begin Sunday school for the Chicago street kids. What an incredible expression of God's love and care for this population.

2. **A.**
   Machen had a difficult time knowing what he wanted to do and finding his purpose in life. He started out at Johns Hopkins and then went to the University of Chicago. After deciding that international finance wasn't for him, his pastor told him to go to Princeton. Although Machen said he didn't want to be a pastor, he enrolled nonetheless.

3. **D.**
   Fosdick was pastoring a Presbyterian church in New York City and was a prominent figure who was featured on the radio and published in papers across the United States. When it was discovered that he wasn't even a Presbyterian, he was removed from office. He continued pastoring and wrote against fundamentalism, promoting liberalism.

4. **C.**
   In 1922, Fosdick preached a sermon called "Shall the Fundamentals Win?" in which he claimed one could be a Christian apart from holding to the fundamentals. Machen published his text in response to Fosdick, arguing that to call oneself a Christian, one must believe the fundamental doctrines of orthodox Christianity.

5. **B.**
Machen saw the need for the church to understand its correct purpose and place. People were coming to the church looking for answers; instead, they found the same chaos and confusion they were experiencing in the world. Because the church had accommodated the culture, there was no true gospel preached. People were not encountering Jesus as the bread of life, which was their greatest need.

6. **A.**
While the liberals may have come in with their wrong doctrine and teaching, they were not the ones doing the most damage. The greatest damage came from the moderates who were striving to maintain unity, peace, and harmony. They would go to great lengths to ensure that everyone was happy and getting along.

10

Evangelicalism, Part 1

INTRODUCTION

Throughout American church history, we have seen an emphasis on doctrine and denominations. Following fundamentalism, the church moves away from denominations to focus more on individual conversion experience as well as the personal study and application of the Bible apart from confessions and creeds. In this lesson, Dr. Nichols sets the stage and explains the key figures and the foundational emphases of the rise of evangelicalism.

LEARNING GOALS

When you have finished this lesson, you should be able to:

- Describe the two main figures of evangelicalism
- Articulate the four main emphases of evangelicalism
- Grasp the importance of the ordinary local church in fulfilling the mission of God

KEY IDEAS

- Evangelicalism was a response to fundamentalism and, largely, the militant separatism it created.
- Carl F.H. Henry and Billy Graham are the two main figures who brought about evangelicalism, each of whom had his own emphases.
- Evangelicalism was rooted in the gospel and non-denominationalism.

REFLECTION & DISCUSSION QUESTIONS

Before the Video

What Do You Think?

Take a moment to answer the following questions. They will prepare you for the lecture.

- How would you describe evangelicalism?

- What do you know about the ministry and legacy of Billy Graham?

Scripture Reading

> *Jesus answered him [Nicodemus], "Truly, truly, I say to you, unless one is born again he cannot see the kingdom of God."*
>
> —John 3:3

- What is the significance of being born again?

During the Video

Answer the following questions while you watch the video. They will guide you through the lecture.

Setting the Stage and Carl Henry *0:00–12:32*

- What is the core of evangelicalism?

- What was Carl Henry's criticism of fundamentalism?

- For which magazine was Henry an editor?

Billy Graham and the Emphases of Evangelicalism *12:32–24:33*

- How did Billy Graham gain such a public ministry?

- What were the four main emphases that characterized evangelicalism?

- Why was activism an emphasis of evangelicalism?

After the Video

Answer the following questions after you have finished the lecture. They will help you identify and summarize the major points.

- What is the opposite extreme of withdrawing from culture?

  If you're in a group, discuss the dangers of falling on either side of this pendulum. How do we guard against either extreme, and what would a balanced, biblical approach look like?

- What were the main emphases of Carl Henry and Billy Graham individually? How did these emphases show themselves in these men's ministries and pursuits?

  If you are in a group, share the benefits that can be seen in the body of Christ as a result of people having different gifts and passions.

- What was the problem with the evangelical notion of Biblicism?

  If you are in a group, discuss the complexities of this idea: on the one hand, God's Word is our authority and gives us everything we need for life and godliness, but on the other hand, God has given teachers and established the community of believers.

PRAYER

Commit what you have learned from God's Word in this lesson to prayer.

- Praise God for the simplicity of the gospel message.
- Confess any ways that you have either removed yourself from our dark culture and not been a light or been too ensnared in the culture and lost your saltiness and distinctiveness.
- Thank God for ordaining teachers who help us understand His Word.
- Ask God that you would center your life around the gospel and faithfully proclaim the gospel to a lost world.

REVIEW QUIZ

Use these multiple-choice questions to measure what you learned from this lesson.

1. The Lutheran church was known as the *Evangelische*. What did that mean?
   a. "The gospel kingdom"
   b. "The gospel church"
   c. "Gospel-centered"
   d. "Gospel culture"
2. When did evangelicalism flourish?
   a. Around the start of the 1900s
   b. The first half of the twentieth century
   c. The second half of the twentieth century
   d. Since the early 2000s until now
3. Who were the two key figures of evangelicalism?
   a. Carl Henry and Billy Graham
   b. Billy Graham and Bob Jones
   c. Carl Henry and E.J. Carnell
   d. Billy Graham and Nelson Bell
4. Who mentored Billy Graham?
   a. Bob Jones
   b. Nelson Bell
   c. David Bebbington
   d. J. Gresham Machen
5. What was "conversionism" a reaction to?
   a. Fundamentalism
   b. Activism
   c. Separatism
   d. Nominalism
6. What did the term *crucicentrism* mean?
   a. "Centered on the church"
   b. "Centered on suffering"
   c. "Christ-centered"
   d. "Cross-centered"

Answer Key—Evangelicalism, Part 1

REFLECTION & DISCUSSION QUESTIONS

Before the Video

What Do You Think?

These are personal questions. The answers should be based on your own knowledge and experience.

Scripture Reading

- What is the significance of being born again?

  According to Jesus in His conversation with Nicodemus, being born again is the only way that a person can see the kingdom of God. Later in the passage, Jesus says a person cannot "enter" the kingdom of God without being born again. Therefore, one's conversion through being born again is of utmost importance. We are dead in our transgressions and sins, needing God to give newness of life, that we might be reconciled with Him through His Son.

During the Video

Setting the Stage and Carl Henry

- What is the core of evangelicalism?

  The core of evangelicalism is the "evangel"—the gospel. It was essentially nondenominational because the gospel transcends denominations. Its primary emphasis was the gospel and the fact that people must be born again.

- What was Carl Henry's criticism of fundamentalism?

  Henry saw much militant separatism come out of fundamentalism, especially in the 1920s–30s. He was bothered by how the fundamentalists had seemingly retreated from the world and established their own subculture. He was concerned that Christians were no longer being effective as light in the world.

- For which magazine was Henry an editor?

  Henry was the first editor of Christianity Today. *The magazine was founded in 1956 by Billy Graham and Nelson Bell, Henry's father-in-law. At first, Henry planned to take a sabbatical from Fuller Seminary for one year to edit for* Christianity Today. *After a few years, he decided to remain as an editor at the magazine, a place where he could be engaged culturally.*

Billy Graham and the Emphases of Evangelicalism

- How did Billy Graham gain such a public ministry?

  In 1949, Graham held a crusade in Los Angeles and thousands of people attended. A news reporter went to the crusade and reported on it. As a result of the story's being published in one of his papers, William Randolph Hearst became interested in Graham because Graham and his story would sell many papers. Hearst saw to it that Graham would be made into a story and make headlines, which is precisely what happened.

- What were the four main emphases that characterized evangelicalism?

  David Bebbington, a British historian, proposed a paradigm to understand evangelicalism through the lens of the following four main emphases: conversionism, activism, Biblicism, and crucicentrism. These were the heart of early evangelicalism. Just as fundamentalism had branches, evangelicalism developed branches with different emphases as well.

- Why was activism an emphasis of evangelicalism?

  In response to the fundamentals withdrawing from culture, Carl Henry wrote The Uneasy Conscience of Modern Fundamentalism. *His book was driven by a desire to see Christians and the church step back into culture and influence it. Similar to the social activism that came out of the Second Great Awakening, there arose a great zeal for missions and missionary endeavors along with activism and social activity.*

After the Video

- How is God's intimate relationship with man revealed in the creation of Adam and in the garden of Eden with Adam and Eve?

  Carl Henry saw a danger in fundamentalists withdrawing from the culture in order to protect themselves from the negative effects of the culture. If you err on the opposite side, however, it will look like cultural accommodation. Dr. Nichols mentioned the danger of salt losing its effect (Matt. 5:13).

- What were the main emphases of Carl Henry and Billy Graham individually? How did these emphases show themselves in these men's ministries and pursuits?

  Carl Henry's ministry was built on his belief that the church was not being a light and needed to be more culturally engaged. He believed Christianity needed to engage with culture and bring Christianity to bear upon culture. Billy Graham was focused on the simple gospel message—"You must be born again." That was the essence of his preaching, and he led crusades where thousands of people would come to listen for days and weeks at a time.

- What was the problem with the evangelical notion of Biblicism?

  The evangelicals believed the Bible as the ultimate authority, but they took it so far as to say teachers were no longer necessary. The problem with this is that the Bible itself describes God ordaining teachers in order to help people better understand His Word.

REVIEW QUIZ

1. **B.**
   Long before evangelicalism came on the scene, there was an emphasis on conversion and being born again. The Lutheran church, which came out of the Reformation, was known as "the gospel church."

2. **C.**
   Evangelicalism began on the heels of World War II and dominated American Christianity throughout the second half of the twentieth century.

3. **A.**
   The two key figures in the story of evangelicalism were Carl Henry and Billy Graham. Henry attended Wheaton College and was an excellent student. Before college he had been a newspaperman and was an expert typist. Billy Graham also eventually attended Wheaton College. They both had disagreements with fundamentalism.

4. **A.**
   Billy Graham began in education by attending Bob Jones College. Bob Jones recognized the dynamic nature Billy Graham had, even as a teenager, and sought to mentor him in the same way Paul took Timothy under his wing.

5. **D.**
   The evangelicals stressed being born again and being followers of Christ. They were against the idea that being a part of a certain church or baptized into a denomination gave you a Christian identity. The emphasis was solely on being born again.

6. **D.**
   David Bebbington used the term crucicentrism *to describe one of the emphases of evangelicalism because it focused on the sacrifice of Christ on the cross and stressed an orthodox view of substitutionary atonement. The term means "cross-centered."*

11

Evangelicalism, Part 2

INTRODUCTION

Considering the beginnings of evangelicalism and its emphasis on gospel proclamation, it seems like the church could have been headed in a hopeful direction. We see, however, a wide variety of responses and emphases as evangelicalism spread throughout its second phase amid significant transformation in American culture. In this lesson, Dr. Nichols explains the various movements of this evangelical coalition and the cultural issues surrounding the responses.

LEARNING GOALS

When you have finished this lesson, you should be able to:

- Describe the second phase of evangelicalism and its various groups
- Describe the key figures and their involvement in evangelicalism
- Grasp the importance of the inerrancy of Scripture

KEY IDEAS

- America underwent a massive cultural transformation from 1968–1972.
- Evangelicalism was a coalition of various movements that responded to American culture.
- The inerrancy of Scripture is a doctrine that must be upheld in the midst of cultural shifts.

REFLECTION & DISCUSSION QUESTIONS

Before the Video

What Do You Think?

Take a moment to answer the following questions. They will prepare you for the lecture.

- As the culture of a nation drastically shifts, how should the church respond?

- What truths of Scripture do you find comforting and anchoring for your soul in the midst of cultural transformation?

Scripture Reading

For the righteous will never be moved; he will be remembered forever. He is not afraid of bad news; his heart is firm, trusting in the Lord*. His heart is steady; he will not be afraid, until he looks in triumph on his adversaries.*

—Psalm 112:6–8

- While we cannot control the culture and sin around us, we can control our response. How does this passage help us navigate cultural shifts?

During the Video

Answer the following questions while you watch the video. They will guide you through the lecture.

Cultural Transformation *0:00–14:14*

- What were some of the events in the mid-sixties to early seventies that led to a massive cultural transformation in America?

- What was the second wave of Pentecostalism in the 1970s, and what was different in its emphasis?

- What was the purpose of the Moral Majority, and who founded it?

The Confessionals and the Authority of Scripture *14:14–24:44*

- What groups made up the evangelical coalition?

- When was the Ligonier Valley Study Center founded, and what was its purpose?

- What changed in the sciences from the 1900s to 1990s?

After the Video

Answer the following questions after you have finished the lecture. They will help you identify and summarize the major points.

- What is primitivism, and when was it on the rise?

  If you're in a group, discuss the dangers of primitivism. Are there any benefits, and if so, what are they?

- What was formed in 1978 that was a significant moment in American church history? What did it accomplish and what was the significance?

  If you are in a group, discuss the benefits of Christians coming together in unity even when they disagree on certain aspects of theology. Could there be any negative effects of this?

- What passage of Scripture did Dr. Nichols say was challenged in both the 1900s as well as in recent times, and what were the issues at hand?

  If you are in a group, discuss how you've been affected by the challenge of the authority of God's Word. Spend some time praying for wisdom navigating gender issues, especially for parents raising children in the midst of the chaos and confusion of the culture.

PRAYER

Commit what you have learned from God's Word in this lesson to prayer.

- Praise God that throughout every era, He has maintained a remnant of His church that holds fast to truth.
- Confess ways that you have given in to fear and worry while watching the transformation of our culture.
- Thank God for the authority of His Word. Without His Word as an authority, we would be tossed about by all the shifts in the surrounding culture.
- Ask God to give you wisdom as you navigate the continuing cultural shifts in our current age.

REVIEW QUIZ

Use these multiple-choice questions to measure what you learned from this lesson.

1. What was the movement that took place among the California hippies?
   a. The charismatic movement
   b. The Jesus Movement
   c. The Pentecostal movement
   d. The primitivism movement
2. Who was a clean-cut musician from the 1950s who was involved in the Hollywood music scene and what would eventually become Christian contemporary music?
   a. Pat Boone
   b. Larry Norman
   c. Hal Lindsey
   d. Randy Stonehill
3. Who was the militant fundamentalist who responded to the hippies and the Jesus Movement?
   a. Jerry Falwell
   b. Jack Hyles
   c. Pat Boone
   d. Pat Robertson
4. What was not a primary cultural issue in the 1970s?
   a. Evolution
   b. Gay rights
   c. Abortion
   d. Racism
5. Who wrote *No Place for Truth: Or, Whatever Happened to Evangelical Theology*?
   a. David Wells
   b. R.C. Sproul
   c. James Dobson
   d. James Montgomery Boice
6. What was the goal of the Seeker Movement?
   a. To seek out people looking for a new church
   b. To market the various groups of evangelicalism
   c. To market the church to make it more palatable
   d. To promote the church as a response to primitivism

Answer Key— Evangelicalism, Part 2

REFLECTION & DISCUSSION QUESTIONS

Before the Video

What Do You Think?

These are personal questions. The answers should be based on your own knowledge and experience.

Scripture Reading

- While we cannot control the culture and sin around us, we can control our response. How does this passage help Christians navigate cultural shifts?

  The passage describes a person who is righteous. Such people don't fear bad news that may come their way because they trust the Lord. They know that whatever comes into their lives will first be sifted through the wise, loving hands of a good Father. As we watch the degrading cultural shifts around us, we do not have to fear. We can trust God and the truth of His Word. We can cry out to Him for wisdom as we seek to process and respond to the various issues that arise almost daily. According to the passage, we can have "firm" and "steady" hearts because they are anchored in a firm and steady God.

During the Video

Cultural Transformation

- What were some of the events in the mid-sixties to early seventies that led to a massive cultural transformation in America?

  The drug and hippie cultures were on the rise. Robert Kennedy and Martin Luther King Jr. were assassinated in 1968. In 1970, the Democratic Convention took place in Chicago. Riots, protests, and the Kent State shootings also took place in 1970 in response to the Vietnam War.

- What was the second wave of Pentecostalism in the 1970s, and what was different in its emphasis?

  The second wave of the Pentecostal movement was the charismatic movement. While the Pentecostal movement stressed the baptism of the Holy Spirit as subsequent to salvation, revealed by speaking in tongues, the charismatic movement emphasized signs and wonders, especially accompanying the preaching of the gospel.

- What was the purpose of the Moral Majority, and who founded it?

  Jerry Falwell founded the Moral Majority in 1979 to address the societal sins of

America. This organization was a political action committee to lobby, pressure, and give voice to the perceived majority in order to counter the measures taken by the minority.

The Confessionals and the Authority of Scripture

- What groups made up the evangelical coalition?

  Like fundamentalism, evangelicalism was a coalition of several different groups. The evangelicals included the charismatic movement, the Jesus Movement, the political wing, the culturally engaged, and the confessionals.

- When was the Ligonier Valley Study Center founded, and what was its purpose?

  R.C. Sproul founded the Ligonier Valley Study Center in 1971, right in the middle of this period of cultural transformation in the late 1960s and early 1970s. Dr. Sproul wanted a place where people could engage with their hard questions and find theological answers.

- What changed in the sciences from the 1900s to 1990s?

  In the early 1900s, the focus was on the hard sciences. Darwinian evolution was the issue at hand. In the 1990s, the sciences shifted, and the soft sciences were emphasized. This led to a focus on issues such as gender identity and sexual identity.

After the Video

- What is primitivism, and when was it on the rise?

  Primitivism is the desire to get back to the pure, primitive church as it was in its original state. The goal is to get back to how the church was in Acts 2 without all the denominational structures. Advocates wanted the Word of God and the ordinances in community and fellowship with other believers without any hierarchy or ministers. This was a part of the Jesus Movement in the 1970s.

- What was formed in 1978 that was a significant moment in American church history? What did it accomplish and what was the significance?

  The International Council on Biblical Inerrancy was formed as a result of confessional evangelicals coming together to stress the inerrancy of Scripture. At a meeting in Chicago attended by four hundred leading evangelicals, the Chicago Statement on Biblical Inerrancy was drafted and signed. This was significant because even though these evangelicals didn't see eye to eye on everything, they agreed that it was of utmost importance to uncompromisingly hold to sola Scriptura. *They knew that if they lost biblical authority, then they lost everything. These evangelicals agreed that they could disagree on how to respond to social issues and yet remain committed to doctrine.*

- What passage of Scripture did Dr. Nichols say was challenged in both the 1900s as well as in recent times, and what were the issues at hand?

According to Dr. Nichols, every age of American culture has challenged Scripture and its authority. In the 1900s, creation in Genesis 1–2 was the issue. In recent times, gender in Genesis 1–2 has become the issue. The American church is constantly facing the question of what authority to follow. We need the grace and strength of God to stand firm upon His Word as our authority.

REVIEW QUIZ

1. **B.**
During the 1970s, Chuck Smith began evangelizing the hippies in California, and many of them came to Christ. The result was the Jesus Movement, which coincided with the charismatic movement.

2. **A.**
Pat Boone was a prominent figure in the Jesus Movement, particularly in the music scene. He was a spiritual father to several hippie musicians, using the pool at his Hollywood home to baptize people.

3. **B.**
Jack Hyles was a militant fundamentalist who was opposed to the hippie culture in America and the Jesus Movement in the church. He responded with a sermon titled "Jesus Had Short Hair," which was published and widely distributed in 1969.

4. **D.**
A number of cultural issues were confronted in the 1970s, including abortion, gay rights, pornography, banning of prayer in public schools, and teaching evolution in public schools. Each of these issues was addressed by Jerry Falwell since he believed America was a Christian nation and under threat of God's judgment as a result of these sins.

5. **A.**
David Wells wrote No Place for Truth: Or, Whatever Happened to Evangelical Theology? *in the early 1990s. In this book, Wells explained the problem with evangelicalism in the 1970s and 1980s.*

6. **C.**
The Seeker Movement was born in the 1980s out of a desire to market the church and make it more palatable to the American culture. It was a response to the fear that the church was being left behind in American culture.

12

What's Next?

INTRODUCTION

We have followed the tale of American church history from its beginning until our present time. In our study, we have seen the consistency of two paths—cultural accommodation and confessional affirmation. In this lesson, Dr. Nichols reviews American Christianity according to the various accommodations made by the church. As he looks ahead and asks "What's next?" he explains the message we can and must cling to as we move forward as Christians who hold to confessional affirmation.

LEARNING GOALS

When you have finished this lesson, you should be able to:

- Briefly explain an overview of American Christianity and the cultural accommodations that have occurred throughout American Christianity
- Analyze the worldly philosophies and false doctrines that pervaded American culture as well as American church culture
- Describe some of the key individuals throughout American church history
- Articulate the foundational doctrines and message of the church

KEY IDEAS

- American Christianity is marked by various periods of cultural accommodation.
- It is essential to maintain an accurate, high view of God.
- God calls His people to a countercultural message, and the gospel must remain the central tenet of the church.

REFLECTION & DISCUSSION QUESTIONS

Before the Video

What Do You Think?

Take a moment to answer the following questions. They will prepare you for the lecture.

- How would you summarize the church history of America?

- What do you think is next for American Christianity and American culture?

Scripture Reading

I [Christ] will build my church, and the gates of hell shall not prevail against it.

—Matthew 16:18

- How does Christ's promise bring rest, hope, and courage?

During the Video

Answer the following questions while you watch the video. They will guide you through the lecture.

Review of American Christianity *0:00–15:09*

- Dr. Nichols explained that learning American Christianity is interesting and instructional but that it can only be instructional if we learn in a certain way. What is necessary for our learning to be instructional?

- What is an accommodation to lukewarm Christianity that was not only seen in the 1660s but throughout every generation of American Christianity?

- Who were some of the key figures of the confessional branch of evangelicalism referenced by Dr. Nichols?

What Lies Ahead? *15:09–25:31*

- What did Dr. Nichols say we do not know about what lies ahead, and what do we know?

- Why can't we think of the church as being inextricably linked to our cultural context?

- In *City of God*, does Augustine say that Christians should not care about what happens in their cultures?

After the Video

Answer the following questions after you have finished the lecture. They will help you identify and summarize the major points.

- What does the following quote by David Wells mean? "God rests far too casually on the shoulders of the American church."

  If you are in a group, discuss ways that we, as individuals and as churches, can grow in our understanding of who God is. How do we keep this vision of who God is central?

- Consider H. Richard Niebuhr's summary of liberalism: "Liberalism taught a God without wrath, brought a people without sin into a kingdom without judgment, through the ministrations of a Christ without a cross." What does this thinking lead to?

  If you are in a group, discuss why we can actually find hope in the truth about God's wrath, man's sinfulness, judgment, and the cross of Christ.

- What matter is at the heart of being a Christian and why?

  If you are in a group, spend some time summarizing some of the most impactful points of this teaching series.

PRAYER

Commit what you have learned from God's Word in this lesson to prayer.

- Praise God for faithfully building His church.
- Confess ways you've been tempted to soften or compromise doctrine because it sounds severe.
- Thank God for Christ and Him crucified, through whom you are clothed in righteousness.

- Ask God to build His church and to raise up men and women who will boldly stand for right doctrine.

REVIEW QUIZ

Use these multiple-choice questions to measure what you learned from this lesson.

1. What was the purpose of H. Richard Niebuhr's *The Kingdom of God in America*?
   a. To show how America was God's nation
   b. To respond to modernism in American culture
   c. To analyze and critique the decades of liberalism
   d. To question whether God had abandoned America

2. When did we see the shifting away from creeds, confessions, and doctrine begin?
   a. During the First Great Awakening
   b. During the Second Great Awakening
   c. During the rise of the early republic
   d. During the rise of liberalism

3. Dr. Nichols mentioned three solas that must be at the core of our identity in order to maintain God-centeredness. Which of the following is *not* one of the *solas* mentioned?
   a. *Sola fide*
   b. *Sola gratia*
   c. *Solus Christus*
   d. *Soli Deo gloria*

4. Which book does Dr. Nichols strongly believe every Christian ought to read?
   a. *City of God*
   b. *The Confessions*
   c. *No Place for Truth*
   d. *Christianity and Liberalism*

5. Which *Pilgrim's Progress* character was J. Gresham Machen identified with by his biographer?
   a. Faithful
   b. The Interpreter
   c. Standfast
   d. Valiant-for-truth

6. True cultural engagement is measured by influence.
   a. True
   b. False

Answer Key—What's Next?

REFLECTION & DISCUSSION QUESTIONS

Before the Video

What Do You Think?

These are personal questions. The answers should be based on your own knowledge and experience.

Scripture Reading

- How does Christ's promise bring rest, hope, and courage?

  It's easy to look at some of the bleak times in American church history, including our current situation, and to become disheartened. Christ's promise to build His church brings Christians glorious rest, hope, and courage. We rest, knowing that God is the One who builds His church. We faithfully serve, but the weight of building the church rests on His shoulders, not ours. We can hope because His church will not be trampled or overcome. We press on with courage, fighting the good fight of faith, knowing the battle and victory belong to our King.

During the Video

Review of American Christianity

- Dr. Nichols explained that learning American Christianity is interesting and instructional, but that it can only be instructional if we learn in a certain way. What is necessary for our learning to be instructional?

  According to Dr. Nichols, we need "eyes to see and ears to hear." We need a willingness to be faithful disciples of Christ now—in this place, in this time, in this moment. To expand on what Dr. Nichols shared, this requires a heart of humility. Only a humble person can learn.

- What is an accommodation to lukewarm Christianity that was not only seen in the 1660s but throughout every generation of American Christianity?

  In the 1600s, it was specifically the "Half-Way Covenant" or "Half-Way Christianity." It is essentially "nominalism" that has been seen throughout every era of Christianity in America. It is a lukewarm Christianity that desires God so long as He doesn't infringe on one's self-interest.

- Who were some of the key figures of the confessional branch of evangelicalism referenced by Dr. Nichols?

  R.C. Sproul, James Montgomery Boice, and David Wells were key figures of the confessional branch throughout the seventies, eighties, and nineties, in addition to John MacArthur. These men were firm in their doctrinal convictions and held to the same doctrines the Puritans stood upon: the holiness of God, God's sovereignty, and God's transcendence.

What Lies Ahead?

- What did Dr. Nichols say we do not know about what lies ahead, and what do we know?

  The truth is, we don't know what's coming. We certainly feel the shifts of culture, but we don't know where it's all leading for our culture or the American church. What we do know is that whatever we're walking through, God has called us to stand through that particular time in our specific place.

- Why can't we think of the church as being inextricably linked to our cultural context?

  Culture is fleeting and is not our anchor. Our anchor is God—who He is, revealed through His Word. We find our identity in the gospel of the Lord Jesus Christ. It is important for American Christians to come to understand this. If we tie the church to our cultural context, what will happen when that cultural context no longer exists, as was the case with Rome? Culture is not a sure foundation to anchor ourselves to.

- In *City of God*, does Augustine say that Christians should not care about what happens in their cultures?

  Augustine argues the opposite. When God saved us, He did not immediately remove us from this world. Rather, He saved us and called us to remain in our specific time and place. He has a purpose for us, and what we do with our lives in this world matters and echoes into eternity.

After the Video

- What does the following quote by David Wells mean? "God rests far too casually on the shoulders of the American church."

  David Wells was referring to the casual approach the American church takes toward God. The church's view of God falls far short of His true character. The church needs a greater vision of who God is—sovereign, holy, transcendent, majestic, and glorious. Without this understanding of who God is at the center of their worship and mission, the church cannot function properly.

- Consider H. Richard Niebuhr's summary of liberalism: "Liberalism taught a God without wrath, brought a people without sin into a kingdom without judgment, through the ministrations of a Christ without a cross." What does this thinking lead to?

  This thinking devalues God and His character, and it elevates man. To believe liberalism is to completely lose the gospel. If God is without wrath, then He is only kind, benevolent, loving, and gracious. If man is good, then there is no judgment. And if there is no need for judgment, then there is no need for the cross of Christ.

- What matter is at the heart of being a Christian and why?

  The cross is at the heart of being a Christian. We preach Christ and Him crucified, which is not possible without a cross. It is through the cross of Christ that we are dressed in His righteous robes, made holy and blameless, and made ready for eternity with God in His very presence. The cross is absolutely central to being a Christian. This transcends time and culture because it is what being a faithful disciple is all about.

REVIEW QUIZ

1. **C.**
   Niebuhr wrote The Kingdom of God in America *in 1937. He offered a helpful and precise summary of liberalism, analyzing its influence in the prior decades.*

2. **B.**
   During the Second Great Awakening, religious populism rose. The church began negotiating with the culture and making accommodations for the American spirit of exploration on the frontier and the Jacksonian democracy. It was during this period that the church started leaving the creeds and confessions behind.

3. **D.**
   We know the gospel through the truth of Scripture, and we rest on sola Scriptura *for our doctrine. At the core of the gospel and our identity, we have* sola fide, sola gratia, *and* solus Christus. *This foundation in the gospel keeps us from becoming man-centered and orients us toward God, which, though not mentioned, helps us maintain* soli Deo gloria.

4. **A.**
   Dr. Nichols believes, while not excluding the other answers, that it would serve every Christian well to read Augustine's City of God. *Dr. Nichols referenced this book at the beginning of the series and commends it again to listeners because it is such a treasure trove of knowledge, and there are many lessons for us to learn today from the book.*

5. **D.**
   Machen's biographer, Ned Stonehouse, referred to him as "Valiant-for-truth" because he stood up for orthodoxy. Machen founded a denomination and started a seminary in order to stand for truth.

6. **B.**
   According to Dr. Nichols, true cultural engagement is confessional, convictional affirmation because without convictions, influence cannot occur. God does not call us to numbers but to faithfulness.